H

Each Lesson That We Learn
Is Like A Few Raindrops

Collectively, They Become
A Sea Of Experience

T.S. Chin

Merry Christmas
Santa 2013

III Edition

H.A.P.P.Y.L.I.F.E.

All Rights Reserved

Copyright © March 2009 by Thick S. Chin

No part of this publication may be reproduced, scanned, translated, transmitted, or distributed in any print, electronic form, or any other format without the written consent of the author.

Any, or all parts, of this publication stored in a database, computer or retrieval system without the written consent of the author is strictly prohibited.

ISBN: 978-0-615-33094-5

Contact the author at:
HappyLifeBook@Yahoo.com

Visit our website at:
http://www.HappyLifeBook.com

Emperor's Choice

At dawn, an ancient Emperor was presented with two pieces of jade as the symbol for his country. One piece was gorgeous, flawless and precious. It was pure treasure. The other was imperfect, filled with cracks and had a worn look. It was difficult to appreciate its value.

The experts and cabinet members in the palace were praising the perfect jade and recommended that it be chosen. However, the Emperor's attention remained on the imperfect jade. The entire palace grew silent.

At dusk, the Emperor made his decision. He chose the imperfect, worn jade and said proudly to his people, "This is the symbol of our country." Everyone cheered.

Philosophers and wise men have debated the Emperor's choice for centuries.

It is time to unlock the Emperor's secret and wisdom. Do you have the curiosity and desire to search for the answer? Everyone has his or her own answer in reference to the Emperor's secret. For more information, please visit our website at www.HappyLifeBook.com.

H.A.P.P.Y.L.I.F.E.

Contents

Foreword

Introduction

Section

(1) **H***elping*

(2) **A***ttitude*

(3) **P***atience*

(4) **P***assion*

(5) **Y***es*

(6) **L***ove*

(7) **I***mprovement*

(8) **F***airness*

(9) **E***ducation*

Special Acknowledgement
Letters From students

H.A.P.P.Y.L.I.F.E.

Section One: Helping

Helping ourselves by helping others is the key to a happy life.

Chapter	Page
(1) I'm Sorry, Mom	22
(2) Tears In A Teacup	25
(3) Thanks For The Handshakes	27
(4) Shoveling Snow Can Be Fun	30
(5) Learning Chinese Chess	32
(6) An Old Lady Brought Back To Life	35
(7) Thick Chin, Short Neck	36
(8) Giving Is Receiving	38
(9) I've Got Food	42

H.A.P.P.Y.L.I.F.E.

Section Two: Attitude

A positive attitude equals opportunity. It will foster positive energy around you, which will lead to success and happiness.

Chapter	Page
(1) My First Appointment	44
(2) No Thanks	47
(3) Four Traffic Violations In One Day	49
(4) Darkness Becomes Daylight	51
(5) The Falling Spider	53
(6) The Soup Was Never Hot	55
(7) A Tax Auditor Listened	57
(8) Our Guardian Angel	58
(9) Free Air	60

H.A.P.P.Y.L.I.F.E.

Section Three: Patience

Patience is your strongest inner power. It is your best tool to conquer fear, obstacles and challenges. Control when and how to act in order to capture opportunity.

Chapter	Page
(1) Waiting For What?	62
(2) My Swollen Knee	64
(3) A Miracle Recovery	66
(4) Raising The White Flag	68
(5) One Patient Parent	70
(6) Pace Makes The Race	72
(7) I Can't Go Fishing	74

H.A.P.P.Y.L.I.F.E.

Section Four: Passion

**If you choose a career you are passionate about, you will never work a day in your life.
Find your passion and live your life in Paradise.**

Chapter	Page
(1) Where's My Tip?	76
(2) Dad Loved To Cook	78
(3) Passionate Politician	80
(4) Passionate People Welcome Busy Days	82
(5) A Cook Who Could Paint	83
(6) Toastmasters Don't Burn	85
(7) Enjoy Your Own Paradise	87

Section Five: Yes

A dream and a plan: anything is possible. Yes we can!

Chapter	Page
(1) A Teacher For Life	89
(2) Moving Mountains	92
(3) Hope With A Plan, "Yes! We Can!"	94
(4) Saying "Yes" To A Stranger	97
(5) Ask Again	99
(6) A "Yes Man" Says "No"	100
(7) The Value Of "Yes"	101

Section Six: Love

Love is caring, educating and sharing openly and unconditionally, without boundaries.

Chapter	Page
(1) My Love Story	105
(2) The Man I Grew To Respect And Love	109
(3) Five People On A Honeymoon	111
(4) Aurea	112
(5) When I Was Sick	114
(6) A Midnight Meal	115
(7) The Ways We Love	117

Section Seven: Improvement

Improve one step each time and improve one percent each day toward your goal and perfection.

Chapter	Page
(1) A Penny A Day	120
(2) Spear Versus Shield	121
(3) Being A Team Player	123
(4) Don't Miss The Handle	124
(5) Mission Accomplished	125
(6) Plan Your Work And Work Your Plan	127
(7) Make Your Own Key	130

Section Eight: Fairness

**Life may not be fair to you,
but you must be fair in life.**

Chapter	Page
(1) A Tough Negotiator	134
(2) Burdensome Emotions	136
(3) The Uncle Who Hit The Jackpot	138
(4) Listen To Our Stomach	139
(5) The Real Estate Sand Trap	140
(6) "It Is Fair, Dad"	144
(7) Why Me?	146

H.A.P.P.Y.L.I.F.E.

Section Nine: Education

Education is the source of knowledge. Sharing knowledge creates a positive rippling effect that benefits mankind.

Chapter	Page
(1) Don't Live In A Home Without A Roof	150
(2) Elephants Teach	151
(3) Turtles Fly	153
(4) Chopsticks	155
(5) Running Out Of Yardsticks	158
(6) A Fable I Once Read	160
(7) Two Heads Are Better Than One	163
(8) Write Your Own Fortune	165

Foreword

We have a mission as human beings: to better our lives and the lives of others. We better our own lives by adopting a positive attitude and striving to improve ourselves. We enrich the lives of others by sharing our experiences, love, cooperation, patience, and passions.

When we are able to apply these principles, the human experience is at its pinnacle. Despite our tragedies, failures, and disappointments, we can always change a negative impact into a positive outcome.

In the spring of 2009, I had the opportunity to speak to the graduating students of a local high school. I was asked to encourage the students to continue their education in whichever way they choose, academically or otherwise.

I accepted this assignment with joy and enthusiasm. My theme, "How to achieve a happy life," allowed me to share my perspective on living a happy life and emphasize the importance of education.

I related my life experiences, wisdom and insight to the students. I encouraged them to have a positive attitude, to share their love, to be patient, to learn, to improve and to find their passion in life.

The appreciation from the students about my presentation moved me to write this book. Although my message has now expanded to a larger audience, my purpose of wanting others to have a happy life remains the same.

H.A.P.P.Y.L.I.F.E.

Life is never meant to be easy. Everyone has his or her own interesting personal stories to tell. Like others, my story tells of obstacles, challenges and a unique life experience.

Despite all the challenges, I remain a happy man. I have learned from my experiences to gain a positive attitude. I have learned how to understand others and to be able to resolve issues. I maintain a positive outlook and enjoy a very meaningful life.

Please join me as I reminisce about my childhood, my journey to America, my life as a young immigrant, and my successes and failures. I will show you how to achieve a happy life through Ancient Wisdom and Modern Philosophy.

I hope that you can discover new perspectives to guide you on your own journey. You will be rewarded with a H.A.P.P.Y.L.I.F.E.

Introduction

I was born in Hong Kong shortly after World War II and was brought up solely by my mother. She treated me like I was her prince, not because we were wealthy, but because I was her only child and the only hope for her future. She could not give me gold or treasures, but she gave me her love and wisdom for which I will always treasure.

At my sixth birthday party my friend asked me, "Do you have a father?" Immediately I snapped, "Does it matter? It's none of your business." I didn't mean to be rude to one of my best friends, but I was a young child who was hurt by this question. My mother was the only parent figure in my life. She loved me and I loved her. I had never met my father.

I had not dismissed the question in my mind as quickly as I had dismissed my friend. A father, did I have one or not? Did it really matter? For days and months, I laid awake at night asking myself these questions. I knew that even if I did not have a father, I still had a great life, and I lived and enjoyed each day. I accepted these facts, but the question continued to burn in my mind. I loved my mother, so I didn't ask her about my father for fear of hurting her feelings.

When I was eight years old, I had the opportunity to go to Phu Ching Middle School, one of the best schools in Hong Kong. As I became more educated, my curiosity about my family peaked.

I asked my mother where she came from, about her family and about my father.

H.A.P.P.Y.L.I.F.E.

I started to learn about her past and my heritage through the captivating stories she would tell. The vivid details she shared with me about her life have stayed with me to this day.

She enlightened me with stories of her childhood, growing up in a World War II embattled nation and enduring unfathomable hardships. To escape the constant bombing and enemy fire, her family traversed the war-torn countryside, climbing mountains and seeking refuge wherever they could.

Many times, her family would pass through abandoned villages that were strewn with corpses and mangled body parts. After several long years, her family returned home to nothing but ash and destruction. Shortly thereafter, the poor and tattered nation of China fell to communism.

For my mother's family this meant the loss of their land, freedom and individual rights. The fear of the unknown made them refugees in their own country. My mother and her family escaped to the former English colony of Hong Kong in search of freedom and better opportunities.

New challenges faced them in Hong Kong as hundreds of thousands of migrants sought shelter and jobs in the underdeveloped city. Families made homes out of sampan sailboats or shared one apartment with several families. It was in one of those cramped apartment buildings that my mother and father met and married.

Finding a job in Hong Kong was just as hard as finding a living space. My father was desperate to provide for his family. He was offered the opportunity to move to the United States. With encouragement from my mother, my father left our family to make a living and provide a better future for us in the U.S. My father promised my mother he would one day bring us to join him. My father left Hong Kong three months before I was born.

After hearing this history, tears came to my eyes. I finally knew that I *did* have a father and I felt a sense of loss that I had not experienced before. I could not wait to meet him, no matter how long it took. I strived to study hard in school. I learned how to write so I could correspond with him. I wanted to impress my father so I practiced my handwriting daily before I wrote a letter. With my mother's help, I was able to send my first letter to him before my ninth birthday.

The life I lived in Hong Kong was very difficult. I never slept in my own bed, as we shared a small apartment with several families. I shared my tiny room with other children. Employment was still difficult to attain and most children wore old ragged clothes because new ones were expensive.

Through those hard times, neighbors bonded together. We treated our friends as if they were family members. We shared our food, our clothes, our hearts and our homes. Their joys and sorrows became our joys and sorrows. Passion and empathy among friends and families kept us together during hardship. There was little crime and people lived in peace, patiently waiting for better days to come.

Better days for me came when I was almost sixteen years old. My mother and I stepped out of the airplane in America, my new country. I raised my head and looked at the sky, the moon seemed to be hanging higher and shining brighter. The sky seemed endless, mirroring the numerous possibilities I had in this country. I breathed in the fresh air and was overcome with a new sense of American freedom.

As I approached the gate, an odd feeling came over me. I knew that this stranger I was walking toward was my father. I was nervous, but once we shook hands and hugged, with tears in our eyes, the unfamiliarity was replaced by love. It was a kind of love I had never experienced before.

I was excited to be in America, not only to meet my father, but also to find a new home in this country. My happy life had begun.

Coming to America, however, did not mean my struggles were over. As a teenage immigrant, I faced difficulty learning the English language and adjusting to a new culture. As an entrepreneur, I have learned valuable lessons through adversity, obstacles and hard work. Our country has also experienced challenges and struggles. During wartime and economic downturns, people have lost money, jobs, health care, homes and loved ones.

These trying times remind me of the economic climate of post-World War II Hong Kong. I remember the hardship we experienced, but I also remember overcoming it too. I know how difficult it is for us to face these kinds of challenges, but I believe that we have the power to conquer these battles as well.

Now that you have heard a bit about my past, it may seem strange that I would know anything about living a "happy life." While I am not claiming expertise, I will use my personal experiences as examples. I am not perfect and I have failed many times, but I have learned from my attempts.

H.A.P.P.Y.L.I.F.E.

I would like to think of myself as bullet proof, not because I am invincible, but because my body is full of holes. I will continue to make mistakes, but I will also continue to learn from them. By overcoming overwhelming obstacles, defeat, personal failures and business disasters in my own life, I have learned that happiness can be attained regardless of the situation. It doesn't matter whom your parents are, where you were born or the hand that you were dealt. I may lose everything I have today, but my pride, confidence, character, love and wonderful experiences will always remain. I will always consider my life meaningful and productive. I will always be happy.

I have outlined several principles herein that describe ways to win personal battles, achieve goals, help others and set good examples for our younger generations.

At the beginning of each section of the chapters, you will be introduced to each principle, as well as some Ancient Wisdom and Modern Philosophy that has guided my writing and my life. Some of these sayings may seem like "common sense," but I have found that common sense is no longer common. You may have heard these principles before, but I aim to offer new perspectives on them. Each principle is illustrated with experiences from my own life.

I hope that you can learn from my experiences. By *H*elping others, having a positive *A*ttitude, exercising *P*atience, fostering *P*assion, saying *Y*es we can, learning to *L*ove, aiming for *I*mprovement, understanding *F*airness and valuing *E*ducation, you can define your own path towards a **H.A.P.P.Y.L.I.F.E.**

Helping

*Helping ourselves by helping others
is the
key to a happy life.*

Ancient Wisdom
"Helping is the root of happiness."

Modern Philosophy
"Giving is receiving."

I'm Sorry, Mom

As I sank deeper into the depths of the reservoir, my mind grew weary. My lungs felt as if they were going to explode from the lack of oxygen. Grabbing the leg of a swimmer above, I tried to pull myself above the surface. We were both struggling to get to the top. I knew I shouldn't have been in the reservoir in the first place.

My mother always told me to stay away from the water because I couldn't swim. As I clung to the flailing swimmer above, I contemplated death. I honestly thought this was the end of my life. My conscience told me to let go and allow the other person to get above the water. If I had to die, why should I take another life with me?

I felt at peace as soon as I released the other swimmer. I knew I had done the right thing. As I felt myself slip out of consciousness, the last thought that flashed through my mind was, "I'm sorry, Mom." All I could think about was how much sorrow I would have brought to my mother because I had disobeyed her advice.

I drifted deeper and deeper, helpless and near death. The other swimmer reached the surface and screamed for help. His screams brought rescuers who pulled us both from the reservoir. Little did I know that the act of letting the other swimmer go (brought on by my mother's lessons of being nice and not harming anyone) would save my life.

By releasing my grip and freeing the other swimmer, I was helping myself get rescued. *I was helping myself by helping others.*

H.A.P.P.Y.L.I.F.E.

I was pulled out of the reservoir. I remember waking in a dark and quiet state of mind, my eyes and ears clouded with water. After an unknown length of time, I gasped for air and regained consciousness. As I settled down, there were a lot of people around me but the people who had rescued me had already left. I never got the chance to thank them.

I walked home by myself, free to reflect on the experience in solitude. I thought about how lucky and thankful I was for the help of those strangers. I thought about my mother and how she had warned me never to swim unsupervised and how I should have listened to her.

From then on, I understood that my mother may say things I might not want to hear, however, it would be in my best interest to listen to her advice, for my benefit.

The unselfish acts of the people that saved my life instilled a moral compass in me that has directed my actions ever since. The effects of that near-death event caused me to commit my life to helping others.

When I was growing up, I was determined to enter a career that helped people. My mother suggested I become a doctor to help people and save lives. She taught me that the most important part of helping others was to do it with kindness and respect.

When I was applying to different schools of medicine, one admissions officer asked me why I wanted to become a doctor. I said, "I have a steady hand, I am a hard worker, I have a nice heart, and I want to help people."

"Son, helping people is important because when someone asks you for help, you may be their last resource," he replied.

As soon as I heard his comment, I felt a chill run down my spine. I took this statement to heart and I learned the importance of lending a hand to others as if I was their last hope.

I never became a doctor (partly because I failed college English. Again, I'm sorry, Mom!). However, that conversation with the medical school admissions officer reaffirmed my belief in helping others. I can serve people and assist the general public regardless of my profession, wealth or state in life.

I started to learn how to show respect, even if it was as little as smiling and saying "good morning" to others. My mini-step of spreading happiness began.

H.A.P.P.Y.L.I.F.E.

Tears In A Teacup

When I receive help, I feel happy. When I help others, I feel happier. I am always thankful for those who have helped me. We all have been in need of help at some point in our lives. Whether we give or receive help, we always find joy and happiness.

Ancient Wisdom says, "Helping is the root of happiness."

Philanthropists donate their time and money to help the needy. I always value their generosity and appreciate their thoughtfulness. I admire them and am encouraged by their contributions. I feel that I can help people in their daily lives by sharing my wealth of kindness and happiness.

By offering a smile, consideration, service and a helping hand to others and the community, I can impact and enrich everyone's life. Financial needs must be met, but spiritual needs are also important. The impact of my goodwill and contributions to the community may be small, but collectively with others, the benefit can be tremendous.

Suppose there was a man who left the office depressed and angry. He had a very unproductive day. His clients yelled at him. His colleagues were disrespectful and his secretary forgot to tell him about an important meeting.

Fuming, he speeds out of the parking lot in his car and onto the highway. Thinking about his horrible day, he swerves in and out of lanes without paying attention. He causes an accident, seriously injuring himself and others.

H.A.P.P.Y.L.I.F.E.

What if you were the last person to see him walking out of the office? What if you had offered him a friendly smile and compassionately asked him about his day? Imagine that the man left the office a little less stressed and he had maneuvered out of the parking lot carefully and drove calmly. No matter how small, an act of kindness can change lives.

I learned how great a small act of kindness could be when three friends entered my restaurant one day. Two of them ordered food while the third young lady sat shaking, with tears in her eyes. I asked her if I could bring her anything, to which she shook her head. I asked, "Is everything alright?"

"She was just in an automobile accident," said her friend, answering for her. "Someone hit her car on the highway and drove away. Her car was badly damaged. She was stuck in the middle of traffic as other drivers continued to speed past her. She was afraid that another car would hit her before the police could arrive to direct traffic."

I fully understood what her friend had just gone through. I expressed my sincere condolences to this young lady. I wanted to comfort her, so I quietly prepared a cup of green tea and brought it to her. I said, "I'm sorry you had to go through such a bad experience. You are in a safe place now. Things will only get better. I hope this tea helps."

Her distressed face suddenly changed. She looked up at me with a genuine smile. Tears slowly fell from her cheek into the steaming cup as she sipped the tea. When I saw her smile, I felt so happy because I knew that I had done the right thing. Sometimes we all just need a small act of kindness, and a cup of tea.

Thanks For The Handshakes

There were many great scholars in Chinese history. Their knowledge and philosophies were well regarded. Their wisdom influenced many generations and benefited many societies and cultures.

I have learned a lot from these stories and teachings. The following story helped guide me through one of my most important challenges in recent years.

One day, Confucius and his students were sightseeing in a town, admiring the marketplace. The marketplace was wet and muddy. The local children played in the mud for fun.

One of the children accidentally ran into Confucius, making his clothing muddy. One of his students witnessed this and pushed the child away from Confucius. The child fell to the ground and began to cry.

Immediately, Confucius kneeled next to the child and apologized. He began to tend to the child and his injury. The student saw Confucius kneeling next to the child and immediately knelt to apologize to both Confucius and the child. They helped the child to his feet and the youngster ran off to play.

On the way back, the student spoke to Confucius, "Sir, you have taught us many things. You taught us to respect and care for our elders. But you never taught us to respect and care for the children in the manner I witnessed today."

Confucius replied, " I have always taught you to respect everyone and that includes children. We must respect all people the same, no matter who they are, where they are from, or what they do. All people are created equal." The students nodded their heads.

Confucius continued, "In fact, we must do even more for our children. We must help them by setting a good example. They are impressionable, so we need to show them how to respect themselves by respecting others. Most importantly, children are our future. We must help them for the betterment of society." The students listened intently and learned a great lesson from the teacher.

This story affected me a great deal. In late March of 2009, I was invited to spend two days to speak to the graduating class of a local high school. I was very excited and felt honored. I knew that this was a great opportunity for me to serve the community and to help guide the students. I had a great responsibility to the students, the teachers and the school.

In order for me to connect with the students, I learned from Confucius that I must respect them. When I came to the class, I felt confident that I would impart the lessons that I had learned in my life.

After I introduced myself, I walked through the classroom to shake the hand of each student, one by one. As I shook their hands, I learned their names to show my respect for them. After shaking their hands and getting to know them, I felt at ease. I knew that I was speaking with friends now, not strangers.

H.A.P.P.Y.L.I.F.E.

I had given the students the respect they deserved. I made my speech to many classes relating my thoughts and life lessons to them. In sharing my perspective of how to achieve a H.A.P.P.Y.L.I.F.E., the students and I had a productive and joyful time.

I had the best days of my life with the students (other than the day I was married and the days my children were born). I was so touched by their support and friendship. When I left the classroom, I knew that I had helped the young people and had made many friends.

Thank you, Confucius, for this lesson. I would also like to thank the students for their warm, friendly and memorable handshakes.

H.A.P.P.Y.L.I.F.E.

Shoveling Snow Can Be Fun

When was the last time you played in the snow? I had never seen snow in my entire childhood. I moved to this country from Hong Kong during the summer. One of the first questions that I asked my father was, "Do we have snow in this country?" His answer was, "Yes." I was so excited and I couldn't wait to see the snow.

To save bus fare, I always walked to my high school, which was located a couple miles away. One morning when I woke up, looking out through the windows, I saw the ground blanketed in a white powder. I had never seen anything like it! The pine trees looked exactly the way they did on those perfect Christmas cards. The scenery was magnificent. I realized this beautiful white powder must be SNOW!

Excited to experience it, I quickly packed my lunch and started my journey to school. I left early so I could play with the snow along the way. As I stepped out of the house, a freezing breeze approached me with snowflakes falling on my face. I loved it!

As I was walking to school, I saw an older couple trying to clear the snow in their driveway with a shovel. I had extra time, so I asked if I could help them to remove the snow. (Mostly because I wanted an excuse to play in it while I shoveled). They happily accepted my offer.

Before I knew it, I had finished clearing the driveway. It was so much fun that I asked the couple if I could do more for them. Although they said no and thanked me, I was happy to have gotten the chance to play in the snow while helping them.

H.A.P.P.Y.L.I.F.E.

    While I was enjoying the snow and the surrounding atmosphere, I noticed that the other children around the corner of the street were throwing snowballs at each other. It looked like they had a lot of fun, so I scooped up a handful of snow and played with it as well.

    As I entered school, I was wet and shivering. It was then I realized that snow could be unpleasant even if you enjoyed playing in it.

    On my subsequent walks to school, I noticed that more and more people in the neighborhood said hello and talked to me. I believe I had made many new friends because the neighbors may have witnessed my good deed of helping the elderly couple. Their friendly smiles made my walks to school a joyful journey each day, and I often forgot it was a long walk.

    My hands were certainly cold that day, but my heart was warm. How can I be unhappy when I had fun playing in the snow while helping others? More importantly, I was able to make new friends.

H.A.P.P.Y.L.I.F.E.

Learning Chinese Chess

Everyone has heard the expression, "giving is receiving." This philosophy is the fundamental theory behind my "helping" principle, "when we are giving, we are receiving."

Let's use the example of helping to motivate a colleague. To do so, we must *give* the following: praise for their accomplishments, credit for their work, and recognition of their contribution.

In return, we will *receive*: a motivated counterpart, improved mutual respect, a friendlier atmosphere, a cooperative work environment, a shared sense of responsibility, increased productivity, and a better outlook for the future.

This simple example and many other lessons teach us that we always receive more than we give to others.

One afternoon, a quiet middle-aged man came to the restaurant and asked me for a job. His name was Hai. I asked him to tell me about the skills that he could bring to the restaurant. He lowered his head and his eyes began to water. "Sir, I'm a refugee from Vietnam," he said humbly. "I have a wife and four children. We have no money, but I do not want to depend on the government for income. I want to work hard to support my family. That is the skill I can bring you."

I was very touched by his personality and determination. While I wanted to help him, I didn't have a need for a new employee at the time. I told him that I could not hire him.

H.A.P.P.Y.L.I.F.E.

He looked at me and said, "Well, that is OK, Sir. If you don't mind, I will come to work for free. I can't get any other job because I don't speak English that well and I am not trained in any skill or trade."

I found myself unable to say no to this passionate man. I could not have him work for free though. I offered Hai a part-time job for a few hours a day three times a week. Every day he was on the schedule, he came in early and didn't leave until I asked him to.

When I asked Hai to clean bar glasses, not only did he work to make the dishes sparkle but he cleaned the entire bar as well. He always went above and beyond in everything he did. The customers raved about his service. He went out of his way to learn the "ins and outs" of my business. Hai was one of the hardest workers I had ever encountered and soon thereafter, I offered him a full-time job.

We continued our partnership for many years and Hai became one of my best assistants. Providing him with employment improved his economic status as well as his knowledge of the English language and the restaurant business. In return, my business thrived with his dedication and hard work.

After working with me for several years, Hai grew to be a great friend. While one of my restaurants was being remodeled, I often came in very early to supervise the construction work.

After a few days, Hai noticed my early arrival in the mornings and asked me if he could come in early to keep me company. I thanked him and told him that it was not necessary, but he came in early anyway.

Hai brought his game of Chinese Chess to help us pass time. We began to play the game daily. The main difference between Chinese Chess and American Chess is that Chinese Chess sets do not have a queen. Hai was an exceptional Chinese Chess player and usually defeated me with ease.

After many days of losing the game to Hai, I asked him to teach me his strategies. Afterwards, I taught the game to my family. Chinese Chess has become a great pastime for us. We have enjoyed the game and our family has grown closer by playing it together.

After only a few days of working with Hai, I knew that my business was going to improve with his employment. Unexpectedly, Hai also improved my relationship with my family, as he taught us how to play his favorite game.

When I was helping others, I was actually helping myself.

H.A.P.P.Y.L.I.F.E.

An Old Lady Brought Back To Life

Do you believe that people can be brought back to life after death? When I was nine years old, my mother and I went to visit my aunt. Upon arriving, my mother, aunt, and cousin went to the grocery store across the street to buy food for dinner. My great-aunt was left at home to watch the children.

As I was playing with some of my young cousins, I heard a thundering crash. I knew something, or someone, had fallen. I ran to find the source of the sound and found my great-aunt lying on the ground. She had collapsed. I ran over and tried to shake her awake but she remained motionless.

Instinctively, I sprinted to the grocery store looking for my family to get help. We returned to find my great-aunt lying on the floor lifelessly. Everyone thought she was dead. Her limbs felt cold and she was not breathing.

My cousin immediately started to resuscitate his grandmother. After a few breaths and several intensive pumps, she coughed and began to regain consciousness. We knew she would live.

I was shocked to learn that my cousin knew how to save my great-aunt. I asked him how he learned those life-saving techniques. He told me that a few months ago he was at a swimming pool when two young swimmers started to drown. There was only one lifeguard on duty, so he was asked to help. He did what he was told and performed rescue breathing on one of the swimmers. Fortunately, both victims survived.

The knowledge that we gain by helping others inevitably helps ourselves in the end.

Thick Chin, Short Neck

My given name in English is Thick Chin. When I was in high school, some of my friends did not call me Thick. Instead, they called me THICK ----- CHIN and the entire class would laugh. I told them, please just call me "Chin"

A few years ago, I had a severe snoring problem. It would wake up my wife and children at night. My family was very concerned about my health. My wife encouraged me to go to a sleep clinic to get a check up.

I was diagnosed with sleep apnea. The doctor told me that I stopped breathing several hundred times each night. They tried to give me an oxygen mask to assist my breathing, but it didn't solve the problem.

Additional tests and treatments were performed without success and my symptoms only got worse. My wife and I began to worry. Ultimately, I concluded that I had a "thick chin and a short neck"! I had to find a solution to help myself.

I started doing stretching and neck exercises, at least three times a day, to help oxygen pass through my breathing channel. As it turned out, it worked! My breathing problem has improved tremendously. I am Thick Chin with a short neck.

I was lucky to figure out the solution to my own problem. Even if others are trying to help you, you must continue to try to help yourself. If you do not want to help yourself, no one else can help you. We have to take some initiative.

A Chinese story illustrates this:

There once was a mother who raised a very lazy son. The mother had to go out of town for a few days to tend to her sister, but she was hesitant to leave her son alone. She hung a very large cookie around his neck to ensure that he was well fed while she was gone.

Upon her return, she found her son lying dead on the floor. The cookie was uneaten. The boy had been too lazy to bow his head and feed himself.

No matter how much other people are willing to help you, if you are not willing to help yourself, you will never be able to benefit from the help of others.

While I have learned how to help others, I have not forgotten to help myself. And, as it happened, I helped others by fixing my snoring problem because I no longer wake up my family!

H.A.P.P.Y.L.I.F.E.

Giving Is Receiving

I learned, as a teenager, to respect and help people, but I really did not understand the saying "giving is receiving" until much later in life. I know if you help people, you will receive happiness and satisfaction. It may only be spiritual, but that is the beauty of it because that is the highest reward that anyone can ever receive, and it cannot be measured by monetary value.

One day, a couple of years ago, I was drafting an economic plan entitled "How to Better America." One of my best friends asked me why I was wasting my time and energy to write something that no one would care to read. I said, "I am just performing my duty as an American citizen. Regardless if anyone reads my economic plan or not, I will send a copy of it to the Congress". Then I told him an interesting story.

There was a terrible drought during the Ming Dynasty. People were lacking food and out of work. Many people were facing poverty, experiencing hunger and were unable to pay their fair share of taxes. Businesses were crumbling, the economy was weak and the country was lacking income revenue.

The King ordered his minister to finance the major businesses in the hopes that the economy could become better stabilized. He also offered a bonus plan to the local government to collect additional tax revenue from the people. The big businesses received the relief, and needless to say, the extra straw placed on the general public was breaking their backs.

H.A.P.P.Y.L.I.F.E.

One summer day, the King was traveling from the palace to his vacation home in the south. In the middle of his trip a man jumped out from behind a bush and quickly kneeled in front of the King's carriage. He was arrested immediately and brought to the King for questioning.

The King was very upset. He exclaimed, "What a disrespectful act! You endangered my safety and interrupted my peace." He turned to a soldier and ordered him to behead the intruder.

The man replied to the King, "Your Highness, I am just a scholar and I will not harm anyone. My life is insignificant, but before I am beheaded, may I say a few words to my King?" The King agreed to hear him speak.

The scholar continued, "For the betterment of our country and the people, *giving is receiving*, my Lord." The King slammed his hand down and said, "Nonsense! Giving is giving and receiving is receiving! Don't you ever try to confuse me!" The scholar said, "My Lord, if I can tell you a story and I am able to prove to you that giving is receiving, would you be willing to listen?" Out of curiosity, the King nodded his head. The scholar told his story:

"Once there was a wealthy farmer who had seventeen cows. He said to all three of his children, 'I am giving my wealth to all three of you. My oldest child gets one-half of my seventeen cows. My second child receives one-third of my seventeen cows, and my youngest boy receives one-ninth of my seventeen cows. There is one condition though, I do not want you to fight over my wealth, and you must receive my wealth with no blood spilled.'

For weeks the children were not able to share the wealth as their father dictated. Often, the discussion resulted in an argument. They could not figure out a way to divide the seventeen cows without cutting some of the cows in half.

Their retired uncle wanted to help and brought in his only cow to the brothers. The uncle said, "I have a cow I want to give you. It's a very old cow but I hope that it can help." The brothers were excited and thanked their uncle for his kindness and generosity.

The oldest brother put the new addition in the lot and took this cow along with eight others and walked away happily, knowing that he received half (nine) of the eighteen cows.

The second brother received his third of eighteen by departing with six cows.

The last brother took one-ninth of the eighteen cows, and strolled away contently with two cows.

As they were leaving, each brother thanked the uncle for his generosity and graciousness. Each brother knew that they had each received their fair share of the wealth from their father.

However, since the cows the brothers had taken totaled the original seventeen ($9 + 6 + 2 = 17$), there was one large, healthy, young cow left for the uncle to take home.

The uncle was extremely surprised, and said, "What happened? I came to help my nephews and give them my old cow, and look what I have received!"

After the King heard this story he said, "That is a very clever story, and I understand in that particular case 'giving is receiving'. But how can this story affect our country and our people?"

The scholar replied, "The people are the foundation of our country and society. They are the ones the King should help first, not the big businesses. The trickle-down effect is just like fixing the roof instead of repairing the foundation. It may look beautiful for a short period of time but ultimately it will fall because we failed to repair the foundation."

The King thought for a moment and then asked, "What are you suggesting?" The scholar replied, "Your Highness, 'giving is receiving', so lower the people's taxes instead of raising them. Create financial assistance by allowing the currency to circulate among the businesses and help the general public improve their productivity. When their livelihoods improve, the tax revenue will also improve. At the end, giving *is* receiving, my Lord."

The King acknowledged his suggestion and allowed the scholar to live. Shortly after, the people received relief from the government and the economy turned around. A long period of peace and prosperity ensued. The tax revenues rose and benefited the country for many years to come.

After my friend heard my story, he asked me, "How do you know that your economic plan will help and benefit America?" I replied, "I do not know. If everyone tries to find the answer before they start a project, the job will never get done. All we can do in life is to try the best we can."

We do what we need to do for the best interest of the people. We may never know what we are going to receive but we are never wrong by continuing to give. Oh, by the way, I did send a copy of my economic plan to Congress.

H.A.P.P.Y.L.I.F.E.

I've Got Food

I love to cook. Do you love to eat? When I first started my restaurant business I was just a teenager, working long hours and facing ever-present loan payments. I was happy because I was thankful to have a job. I knew that if I worked hard, I could provide for my family and my younger brother. If nothing else, I had food.

If you visit my restaurant, you can be sure you will not leave hungry because I've got food. I love providing my customers with heaping portions because I enjoy making them happy and satisfied. When I see a happy face, I feel joy in my heart.

When friends and family visit me at my restaurant, I am happy to provide a meal "on the house" to them. I may not have a lot to offer but I certainly have food. When you are willing to give, you feel rich in your heart.

I like to make people happy in any way I can. Be it a simple smile to a stranger or a free meal, I am glad to help. I have made many great friends and, in return, I have enjoyed an even greater satisfaction.

One of my friends once told me there is no such thing as a free lunch. So I invited him to my restaurant! He doesn't say that anymore. Share your food, whether it's a pack of peanuts or some popcorn. By sharing, you will find satisfaction and happiness.

I always want to find happiness. The best way to do it is by going out to help others. Even if it is just offering a smile or a few kind words, I always find that I am helping myself by helping others.

H.A.P.P.Y.L.I.F.E.

Attitude

*A positive attitude equals opportunity.
It will foster positive energy around you,
which will lead to
success and happiness.*

Ancient Wisdom
"The sun will always rise out of darkness.
There is always tomorrow."

Modern Philosophy
"A positive attitude will change your life."

H.A.P.P.Y.L.I.F.E.

My First Appointment

Several years ago, I was appointed by our state Governor to serve as an Economic Workforce Councilman. I was honored to serve in that capacity. But among all of my life experiences, none had influenced me as much as my first appointment as Class President, by my schoolteacher, Ms. Leung.

As a fifteen year old, my first priority was soccer and school came second. I spent more time at the soccer field than I did studying. I played soccer in the morning before school and I was always one of the last students to arrive in the classroom. I usually ran into the class right before the bell rang with sweat dripping down my face and my shirt soaked.

During school, I found myself thinking only of our next match, and I usually used instruction time to talk to my friends about new plays. After school, I played soccer until it was time for dinner, leaving little time for homework. Needless to say, I was a mediocre student at best.

One morning, my teacher announced that she had appointed someone to be the President of the class – *me!* I was shocked and embarrassed. Traditionally only the best student could receive such an honor. I felt uneasy about the task. I wanted to continue my all-day soccer schedule and not have to worry about the responsibilities of Class President.

I told my mother I did not want to accept the position. She would not let me decline it and told me an ancient story of two heroes:

H.A.P.P.Y.L.I.F.E.

Two friends were sitting in a peach garden. The first, Cheung Fai, was a talented fighter but very short-tempered. The other, Quang Wan Chung, was very honorable, honest, knowledgeable and wise.

"You are such a great warrior," Quang said to Cheung. "But you have to change your attitude or you will never be a celebrated General."

"I am who I am, and I happen to be one of the best fighters in the world," Cheung retorted.

"Well if you don't use your mind, you cannot achieve even the smallest feats in life, regardless of your physical ability," Quang said. "I bet you cannot even kill the ant on this bench."

Cheung extended his thumb toward the insect. Before he could act any further, Quang spoke.

"Before you try, I would like to bet you. If you kill this ant, I will be your servant for the rest of your life. But if you don't and the ant remains alive after your attempt, you must listen to me for the rest of your life."

At this challenge, Cheung became furious. "You underestimate me!" he cried out. With a heavy blow, he slammed his fist onto the bench on top of the ant.

The ant remained unharmed. "You see? You let your emotions blind your actions. Power alone does not get you anywhere," Quang said. "You could have killed the ant with the force of one finger, which you were going to do before I upset you. Instead, you used the force of your fist. The ant survived because your fist could not crush into the grooves of the bench like your finger can. Sometimes we need to change our attitude before we unleash our power." Cheung humbly listened.

"You see," my mother, said, "the hero changed his attitude because of one small lesson. This is your testing time. You must accept this position, but you need to change your attitude and behavior first. You must study harder and take on more responsibilities to improve yourself and set a good example for others."

I followed my mother's instructions and became President of the class. I stopped running in the hallways. I tried to control my talking during class (I just talked more before and after), and I began to act like a gentleman instead of a spoiled child. As time progressed, I became a better student and a better person.

I took the opportunity to take on more responsibility, which changed my attitude and behavior, and led me to success and happiness.

No Thanks

My mother was a great parent and also my greatest mentor. One day, when my mother became very ill, I sat next to her and tried to comfort her. I told her how much I loved her and thanked her for all the caring, teaching and love she had given me.

She held my hand and said, "You have developed a very good personality and a very positive attitude, but you need to work on your patience." I thanked her for her wisdom and told her that the lessons she taught me (such as respecting people and treating people kindly) had fostered many positive and happy experiences that shaped my personality, character and attitude.

She then told me a new story. During the Second World War, many people escaped their villages and went to other cities and towns to avoid the enemy. One traveler knocked on a door and asked for food and clothing. The servant reported this event to her master and asked what the master wanted her to do. The master said, "Go ahead and give him some food and a blanket."

The next morning, they found the man dead beside the house. The food was uneaten and the blanket had not been used. There was a note next to the body. The note just said, "No Thanks."

The master asked the servant about what had happened. She said, "This is wartime. I was afraid he was a bad person, so I threw the food and blanket to him instead of handing them to him. I guess that's why he was upset and did not accept our help."

The master turned his head and told the rest of the family, "We wanted to help him, but by disrespecting him we injured his dignity. He decided to reject our help and would rather die."

My mother continued, "Because of the war, I never had a chance to finish elementary school. While I was a refugee, my father told me stories and fables to give me hope and build my spirit to face challenges." These stories that my mother told me are the ones I am sharing with you in this book.

Regardless of what situation we are in or how we feel, we must maintain our respect for others and treat all people well. Many people face an uphill battle in life, myself included. During these difficult times, we must maintain a positive attitude. When we are helping others, we must be aware of their feelings. We should assist everyone with respect and sincerity.

H.A.P.P.Y.L.I.F.E.

Four Traffic Violations In One Day

One day during college I was late for class so I parked in a two-hour parking zone. At the end of the day, I returned to my car to find four separate tickets for the same parking violation. I marched to the Transportation and Parking Services building and complained. They told me I had to pay them. I paid the first ticket but refused to pay the rest.

At the end of the month I was charged not only for the three additional tickets, but also late fees and processing charges. My negative attitude caused me more hardship.

A month later, there was a fundraising event for the fraternal brothers of the Police Department. The Chief of Police was speaking at the event. Needless to say, after my "quadruple" ticket, I was not a fan of the Police Department.

"Why aren't you going?" my mother asked me. "I already donated enough money to the Police Department with my tickets," I said.

"This event and your problem with your traffic tickets are two different issues. You must take these matters and separate them from personal feelings." She also explained to me that the police were only doing their job to serve the community. I should hold their service in high regard and respect them.

I changed clothes, went to the fundraiser and made a donation. Even though I continued to disagree with my fine and ticket issues, I have changed my attitude toward our law enforcement officers. I have had the utmost respect for them ever since.

H.A.P.P.Y.L.I.F.E.

Several years later, I was stopped by a police officer for an expired inspection sticker. As the officer approached me, I saw, in my mirror, an 18-wheel truck fast approaching us. For the safety of the officer, I moved my car slightly to the right to avoid a possible collision with the truck.

The policeman pulled his gun and yelled, "Stop! What are you doing?" I stopped immediately and pointed at the truck as it nearly missed us both. Without my explanation he understood. He asked me if I knew that my inspection sticker was expired. I told him that I was sorry and that I didn't know. I said, "I'm always a day late and a few dollars short". We both laughed.

It was at this time that I realized we often have misunderstandings among people because either we don't communicate well with each other, or we view things differently and have different opinions. My ability to understand why the policeman pulled his weapon was directly related to the positive attitude I had developed over the years.

When an unpleasant experience makes us angry, it is very difficult to separate it from other events. This causes anger to cloud all aspects of our lives. We must learn to isolate our anger so that we can better manage it. We must extinguish our anger quickly instead of letting it burn out of control.

We must learn how to understand each other's position and the reasons behind their thinking and actions so we can react accordingly with a positive attitude and mutual respect.

H.A.P.P.Y.L.I.F.E.

Darkness Becomes Daylight

Franklin D. Roosevelt once said, "The only thing we have to fear is fear itself." When you break it down, fear is simply the unknown

When we are afraid, it's because we do not know the outcome of an issue or the consequences of the unknown. Once we understand the facts of the situation, we are comforted with our ability to cope with the unknown in any circumstance.

When I was young, my mother often asked me to run errands for her when she was not feeling well. One day I was sent to the drugstore ten blocks away. It was getting dark and I was scared of the narrow alleys. Face red, sweat beading and breathing heavily, I ran back home. I unlocked the door and sprinted into my mother's room.

"What happened to you?" my mother asked.
"I ran home because I was afraid. I thought there was something chasing me, like a ghost," I replied between gasps of air.

She smiled, "Are you a good boy?"
"Yes."
"Did you hurt anyone or do anything wrong?"
"No."
"You see, you are a nice person," she said. "There is no reason for anything to hurt you. You always help me with my errands. There is no need to be scared. Nothing is out there."

The next time I went out to the drugstore, I strolled through the alleys without fear.

H.A.P.P.Y.L.I.F.E.

  The thing we most fear is the unknown. I did not know what was lurking in the alleyways and was scared. After my mother explained that there was nothing that could hurt me, I had no fear anymore.
  Times of unstable economy and uncertain job security are two unknowns that many of us fear in our lives. We need to remember that if we lose everything today, we may start anew with much less pressure and expectations. We may not know how our financial situation may be in the future, but we do know that with a positive attitude, we can overcome anything.
  Have no fear!

H.A.P.P.Y.L.I.F.E.

The Falling Spider

Most children are hard workers and good students. When I was young, I was one of those hard workers but I was a lazy student sometimes. My attitude changed when I heard an ancient story.

One rainy afternoon, a wise man and three of his students ran to a house with a hanging canopy to avoid getting wet. Soon they discovered a spider that kept trying to repair its web. After many attempts, the spider's effort never materialized because the rain kept destroying its web.

The wise man witnessed this and asked his students for their thoughts. The first student said, "I feel sorry for the spider. He tried so hard but failed each time. If it had been me, I would have given up long ago."

The second student said, "I am sorry for the spider too, but he needs to be smarter. He should have waited for the rain to stop or he should have spun a new web in a dry area. I have learned that I need to think more and be smarter in the future."

The third student said, "I admire the spider's endurance and determination. Its will is unyielding. The spider has inspired me to be stronger, endure more and work harder to attain my goals."

The wise man smiled and said, "Excellent!" He turned and pointed to the corner of the house and said, "Do you see that ant? He is carrying 20 times its body weight over a great distance to bring food to his family. If the ant can do this much, as human beings, we can do even more."

The students were confused. The wise man said, "We need to think deeper, smarter, and try harder. We should also apply the lesson we learned from the spider's attitude and perseverance to never give up on anything we attempt to do. The spider will never stop working on his endeavor and we will not be here to see the fruits of his labor. Having practiced and repaired so many times before, perhaps tomorrow he will build a more beautiful and intricate web. Perhaps he will build part of it in the rain. But even if he fails to build this particular web, the practice and perseverance will serve him greatly in the future, as he will be able to build more durable and better webs. The ant is very strong, but humans are even stronger because we have a beautiful mind inside of us." The students were listening carefully.

The wise man continued, "We will construct things in the future that can carry ten times more weight than our own, just as the ant can, and accomplish even greater things than the mind can imagine today. But if we quit now and allow difficulties to stop us, just as the rain does to the spider, we will never accomplish anything. We must have perseverance and utilize our intellectual ability to move us forward"

Soon thereafter dollies were invented, then rolling carts, and then forklifts. Now we have trains, planes and space shuttles.

As the wise man shows us, the observation of the falling spider and the hard-working ant illustrates that nothing is impossible. All we need to do is to search for the hidden meaning to discover the true lesson.

H.A.P.P.Y.L.I.F.E.

The Soup Was Never Hot

Once we learn to control our attitude, it is our obligation to help others cultivate a positive mindset. Changing other people's attitudes is equally as important as changing your own.

Have you ever noticed that when people with positive attitudes surround you, you tend to become more optimistic? Likewise, when the people near you have negative attitudes, you quickly become pessimistic. Encouraging others to adopt positive attitudes will breed happiness.

I once had a customer at my restaurant named Henry. He patronized my business three or four times a week for over a year. Henry was one of our most loyal customers.

There was just one problem. He complained about the food every time he ordered. He complained that the soup was not hot, there wasn't enough chicken in his entrée, the rice was too dry or his egg roll needed more shrimp.

At first, I tried to go out of my way to please him, but his complaints were so regular that I eventually accepted them as a part of serving him. I understood he didn't mean what he was saying. If he were actually unhappy with our restaurant, he would not have returned as often as he did.

One afternoon, Henry came in and proceeded with his usual complaints. He told me that the soup he had during his previous visit was not hot enough. I knew this couldn't have been true because I had made sure that the soup was heated to a boil before we served it.

When Henry had almost finished his meal, I sat down next to him. "Henry," I said, "I want to thank you for your business. You are a great customer and I appreciate it. I want to treat you as my friend."

He nodded and said, "Thank you." I continued, "Because I am your friend, I want to know if there is any way I can make you happier while you are in my restaurant."

He was surprised and said, "What do you mean? I am very happy here."

"Because you complain every time you walk in the door! I want to make sure that you are happy and that's why I ask you how can I improve my business, so that I can ensure that you always leave here happy."

"Oh, no, there is nothing wrong with your food and service," he said. "I really enjoy you and your restaurant!" I smiled. "Thank you so much, you make me feel happy. I love being your friend," I said to him. From that day on, he never complained in my restaurant.

Through open dialogue and sincerity, Henry was able to realize his negativity and change his attitude. By adopting a positive outlook, Henry and I were able to develop a happy relationship and he continued to patronize our restaurant for many years to come.

We want to change other people's attitudes or our own, because we care. When Henry's attitude changed, it fostered a mutual respect between us. Honesty and sincerity will break barriers. When we think positively, we are able to gain respect from others and for ourselves. A good attitude will adjust any temperature.

H.A.P.P.Y.L.I.F.E.

A Tax Auditor Listened

A few years ago I was called into the Department of Taxation for a random audit. I arrived promptly for the nine o'clock meeting. My auditor met me in the waiting area and led me to a meeting room. To her surprise and anger, the door was locked. There was a junior officer working in the room.

"I reserved this room," she bellowed, "GET OUT!" He quickly packed his belongings and scurried out of the room. She slammed the door behind him.

I knew this was not going to be a good day for any of us. "I guess by seeing me, your bad day begins." I said to her. She flashed me a menacing look that dared me to continue.

"I don't mean to be impolite, but the reason you are a senior auditor is because you are smart and have more experience," I said. "The other young gentleman that was in your reserved room may be just learning. I hope you can forgive him for not knowing that the room was reserved."

She smiled for the first time. She excused herself politely and walked out of the meeting room towards the junior auditor. I could only assume that I changed her attitude because she went to apologize to the young man. Shortly after she returned, she pulled her chair up next to mine and we started the meeting. During the audit, she was very professional and found no problem with my taxes. I guess I could say that when I have a positive attitude, I have no debt in life.

When our hearts are in the right place and we are sincere, people will sense our good intent. They will understand and appreciate our positive attitude.

Our Guardian Angel

Good news happens to all people and bad news can happen to everyone too. A few years ago my daughter-in-law gave birth to my first grandchild. He was born incredibly premature, weighing only a little more than one pound. Under the best possible care, he fought resolutely for his life. He gave us more hope with each day that he battled. He made our family closer than ever before.

Unfortunately, after thirty days, he lost his fight. We were all extremely distraught. Disbelief, pain and sadness flowed throughout all of our family's hearts. As the patriarch of the household, I tried to comfort my family as best I could. I offered my love, support and strength. We consoled each other by sharing our love, sorrow and passion.

We eventually learned to cope with our loss and began to smile again. We realized that in losing a grandchild, we gained a guardian angel. We accepted this unfortunate event as part of life. In doing so, our family was able to understand and overcome this tragedy together.

One pleasant summer day I was talking to a customer. "Today is a beautiful day," he said, looking out the window. "I wish we would have more days like this."

After some contemplation, I told him, "Unless we have bad weather, we will not learn how to appreciate the good." Joyful days may come between unpleasant days. When we experience good days, they are more valuable and we appreciate them more.

H.A.P.P.Y.L.I.F.E.

A year after the heartbreak of my first grandchild's death, my son and his wife welcomed another child into the world. He was born full-term, healthy and happy. We are so thankful to have him in our lives, and we have grown to learn how precious he truly is.

My wife and I visit him nearly every day. We love caring for him, playing with him and making him laugh. In experiencing the unpleasant days after our first grandson's death, we are able to fully appreciate the beautiful days with our second grandson.

Regardless of whatever happens in our lifetime, things happen for a reason and for a better purpose. We will always be able to improve our lives by learning how to deal with our tragedy and cope with our losses. Having a positive attitude is essential to foster unity, love and support of our family and friends.

Free Air

A positive attitude is essential for us to have a happy life. When we improve our attitude, we are more willing to help others. By being positive, we can act with patience, work passionately and love more deeply.

Attitude is the common denominator of every other life principle in this book. It is important for us to understand that a positive attitude is critical to successfully mastering all of the other principles.

When we have a positive attitude, we help the people around us have a better outlook on life. That rippling effect changes our lives and the lives of many others.

Our attitude affects not only our actions, but also how we think. It is incredibly difficult to maintain a positive attitude during hardships in life. Controlling our attitude is a learning process that challenges us intellectually, emotionally and physically.

Ancient Wisdom says: "The sun will always rise out of darkness." A modern interpretation of that proverb is "There is always a bright side to life."

We must consider ourselves fortunate because we can improve our lives by changing our attitude. When we do, we are able to look at any situation from all angles.

I have found the best way to foster a positive attitude is to start the day with the right mindset. When I wake up in the morning, I take a deep breath and say "Thank you. I just got free air!" I always find that starting the day off with a positive attitude will make me a happier person.

H.A.P.P.Y.L.I.F.E.

Patience

*Patience is your strongest inner power.
It is your best tool to conquer fear,
obstacles and challenges.
Control when and how to act in order to
capture opportunity.*

Ancient Wisdom
*"Patience, patience, and more patience.
That is the golden rule."*

Modern Philosophy:
"Patience is a virtue."

Waiting For What?

Many people consider the word "patience" to be synonymous with the word "waiting". I, on the other hand, believe that patience requires more skill than simply sitting around and waiting. Patience is all about proper timing.

I was a pre-med student in college. In an attempt to impress medical schools on my applications, I took classes that would boost my grade-point average. This meant taking extra math and science classes and holding off on taking any English classes until it was absolutely necessary.

During the second semester of my senior year, I was forced to take a 300-level English class called "Fiction and Film." I needed to pass this class in order to graduate and start applying to medical schools. Learning English as a second language and having never taken a college writing course, I failed dismally.

Years later I heard a joke about a man who found himself in a torrential rainstorm. As water rose and flooded the streets, he yelled for help. A piece of plywood floated past him. He thought, "I know God will take care of me, I don't need this piece of wood."

The water rose to his chest, and he sought refuge on his roof. A man in a boat came by and offered to save him, but he declined. "I know God will take care of me," he said.

Water then rose up to his neck, so he climbed a tree. A helicopter noticed him and hovered so that he could climb aboard to safety. He again declined.

H.A.P.P.Y.L.I.F.E.

The water continued to rise, and he drowned. In Heaven he met God and asked, "Lord, why didn't you save me?"

God replied, "I did! I sent you a piece of plywood, a boat and a helicopter! What were you waiting for?"

I wish I had heard this story when I first began signing up for classes as a freshman. I waited until the last possible opportunity to enroll in an English class. Looking back, I'm not sure what I was waiting for.

I should have taken English classes earlier so that I could have gradually improved my English skills and knowledge.

Since then, I try not to waste my time waiting for anything. Even though I have learned to be patient, I have to know when to exercise my patience and how to act with my most powerful inner strength to capture opportunities.

My Swollen Knee

In many circumstances, acting impatiently makes our situation worse. I was once playing soccer in Hong Kong when my kneecap was kicked and swelled to the size of a baseball.

I was fearful of telling my mother because I didn't want her to worry about me. Even though I was in pain, I was anxious to continue playing because I enjoyed playing soccer so much. I played the following day because I didn't want to sit on the sidelines. With a lot of pain, I played the following day, as well. By the end of the week, I couldn't walk.

My mother took me to the doctor and we were told that I would not be able to play soccer for a few months. Several weeks went by and I was able to walk again. I asked my mother if I could go outside and play soccer since I was feeling better. In her typical fashion, she told me a story that explained her answer.

There once was a young boy who wanted to learn how to shoot the bow and arrow farther than anyone else. His father forbade him to shoot his arrows and insisted that he build his strength through exercise and lifting weights.

After several months, the son disobeyed his father and went out to the field to shoot. His arrow traveled fifty yards. He returned to boast to his father. The father was not impressed.

"I thought you wanted to be the best! There are others who can shoot the arrow 100 yards. I told you not to shoot yet because you are not ready. If you had waited, you would have been strong enough."

H.A.P.P.Y.L.I.F.E.

He told his son that he needed to continue to build his strength for a few more months.

Once the father knew that his son was ready, he entered him in a State shooting competition. The son cleared 100 yards, winning the contest easily.

Impatience prevents us from fully understanding our situation. In order to move forward like an arrow, we have to first pull back like a bow. In my case, I listened to my mother. I waited a few more weeks and didn't play soccer until I was fully recovered.

As it has been said, "time is the best medicine." Time will heal us both emotionally and physically as long as we can incorporate patience with a positive attitude.

A Miracle Recovery

Patience is closely related to attitude. In a situation that requires patience, it is very easy to become frustrated and pessimistic when you have a negative outlook. Frustration will not get you anywhere in life. Alternately, when you approach the situation with a positive attitude, you grow to be patient. When you combine a positive attitude with a great deal of patience, you get results.

My father was diagnosed with cancer when he was forty-five years old. The cancer specialist at St. Mary's Hospital gave us a bleak diagnosis. My father had only four to six months to live. Running out of options, I remained hopeful and patient.

The doctors told us they would do anything they could to make the remainder of my father's life as comfortable as possible. With hope and love, I asked the doctors to offer my father any treatment that would help him live. As the Chinese proverb says, "You must treat a dying horse like a live one, in order for him to have a chance at survival."

Instead of giving up on my father's illness and enrolling him in hospice care, the doctors administered a series of chemotherapy treatments. My father became weaker, but we remained hopeful. Considering the late stage of the cancer, the doctors were unsure that their attempts would be fruitful.

On the other hand, I was hopeful and had faith that my father could overcome his challenges and be able to get well. I continued to love and support my father. I endured pain in my heart as he was enduring agonizing radiation.

H.A.P.P.Y.L.I.F.E.

Several months later, the doctor asked my father and I into his office. He told us that, after a series of treatments and tests, it was confirmed that my father's cancer had unexpectedly gone into remission. We were so excited and felt so joyful about this great news. We could never thank the doctors enough. I believe that my father had fought hard for his life because he sensed our hope, love and support.

My father was released from the hospital. He recovered quickly and went back to work a couple of months thereafter. He lived twenty-five more healthy, productive and happy years.

We can never expect miracles in life, but we can never give up believing in them. Loving, sharing and caring for our loved ones, in good and bad times, are the best gifts in life. When we are patient, have a positive attitude and are hopeful with love, miracles can occur.

Raising The White Flag

Patience helps you accomplish your goals and achieve a better life, but it requires sacrifice and surrender in order to fully benefit from the power of patience.

An athlete must sacrifice his time, energy, and perhaps the income from endorsement deals while overcoming an injury.

My family surrendered to the fact that my father had cancer and looked for ways to defeat it.

There is an old Chinese proverb that says, "We must die to become alive." When we sacrifice and surrender, we are able to come to grips with our circumstances and focus on how to move forward with a new plan for a better future. We can adjust and set new goals while pursuing new solutions to our problems.

My son John started a computer business when he was in his early twenties. After a few successful years, he came to me distraught.

"One of my biggest clients is declaring bankruptcy. They owe me thousands of dollars and now cannot pay their debt." He asked for my advice. I told him to be patient and not to lose hope. My son agreed.

A couple of weeks later, I asked him how his business was doing. He told me that he would not be receiving any outstanding payments from the bankrupt company. "That is understandable," I told him, "but you should continue your business relationship with this company." I suggested he write off the previous balance and start anew.

We understood that even as this company was surrendering by filing for bankruptcy, they were reorganizing and regrouping. After coming out of bankruptcy, the company still needed John's services. Forgiving the overdue bills would not help John's financial situation, but it would help this company in need. In turn, this company, after the reorganization, would be more willing to do business with John in the future.

We should always work towards new opportunities. John's business blossomed by working with this once-bankrupt company and forgiving the company's debts and his risk paid off. He thought logically and acted with courage, but it required him to sacrifice. Not only was he patient with the bankrupt company, he was also patient with his own circumstances. John was able to turn a negative situation to a positive outcome. His business prospered and he is a happy man.

When facing challenges, it never benefits anyone to panic and run. Only through a thoughtful process and the will to meet challenges with patience, can one find success in failure.

One Patient Parent

Having patience and sacrificing often translates into enduring a period of hardship. My father had to tolerate many doses of painful chemotherapy treatments before he recovered. John endured a period of economic strife while his customer was bankrupt. Patiently enduring hardship will prime you for success.

I met Jason in 1995. I was at the peak of my business success and wanted to "pay forward" by investing back into society. I started a non-profit company called Asian American Consulting Group. The company's mission was to help individuals and small businesses become more successful in our area.

Jason applied for a job at my consulting company. During my interview with him, he told me that he left his family and his country to pursue a Masters degree abroad, then moved to America to start a new life. His story mirrored my father's journey in life. I hired him for part-time work.

Due to the lack of hours I could offer him, he had to take another job to support his family and save money to bring them to America. One day I asked him why he wanted to stay here while his family was so far away, and if all the hard work he was doing was worth it.

"I do it for my son's future and for my family. One day I want my son to come to the United States to have freedom, see the world and get the best education possible. That is my goal," he said.

H.A.P.P.Y.L.I.F.E.

Through his hard work at my company and his other job, he was able to improve his English and customer service skills. He saved enough money to help his family to move to the States.

Now he works for a national retail chain as a general manager and is regarded as a great leader in the company. His son is doing well adjusting to the American culture, finding new friends and excelling in school.

By enduring long hours and working hard, Jason was able to exceed his goals. I respect his courage, patience and accomplishments in this country. He reaffirmed my belief that if we work hard and are willing to sacrifice, success is waiting for us.

H.A.P.P.Y.L.I.F.E.

Pace Makes The Race

I always enjoyed playing soccer but I was never on a track team. When I was in the eighth grade, I saw an announcement in school that the soccer field would be closed due to a track and field competition. My friends and I were disappointed since soccer was our passion and we were unable to play during the track event.

Since I couldn't play soccer, I signed up for the track competition and decided to participate in several events. On the first day, I was in the 200-meter race. When the gun sounded, I sprinted away quickly. I took a long lead and thought that I would win by a big margin. Suddenly, I ran out of gas and slowed to a walk, finishing last.

After the race was over, I could not speak to anyone because I was gasping for air. A moment later, the track coach approached me and said, "Son, you can run. What happened out there? You just stopped." I was so embarrassed and said, "I tried too hard too soon and I just ran out of air."

He said, "You are a fast runner, you just need to control your own pace. I noticed that you were signed up for the 400-meter race tomorrow. Do you think you will be up to it?" I said, "I guess not, Coach, since I could not finish a shorter race."

The coach said, " A 400-meter race is two and a half laps around the inner track. I suggest that you expend seventy percent of your energy in the first lap, ease back just a little bit more in the second lap, and finish the last half lap with one hundred percent of your effort to the finish line."

The coach continued, "The most important thing is not to compare your running position and the distance between you and the other runners during the race. Remember 'pace makes the race' and you must run at your own pace to finish as strong as you can."

The next morning when I was lining up for the 400-meter race, I had a lot of confidence about myself. When the gun fired and the race began, I sprinted forward a little and then slowed down exactly as the coach told me. I followed his instructions perfectly. In the last half lap, I sprinted home with everything I had. I finished extremely strong and ran a powerful race.

Afterwards, the coach approached me and said, "You did a great job!" I said, "I want to thank you for your advice. It's hard to believe that I could finish a 400-meter race so well, since I could not even finish a 200-meter race." He said, "Do you remember that I told you 'pace makes the race'?"

During my adulthood, I have applied this principle of running my own race and the philosophy of not comparing myself with others along the way. I just work as hard as I can with the best pace possible in all of my endeavors.

Sometimes people tell us that our neighbor's or our friend's "grass" is "greener" than our own. We need to remind ourselves that it is best for us to focus and do the best we can in our own life and not to compare ourselves with others.

We can enjoy what we have and be happy regardless of the state of our lives or our own circumstances. We need to set attainable goals, control our own pace, never quit and finish strong.

I Can't Go Fishing

One day, one of my best friends, Eric, asked me to go fishing. I said, "I can't go fishing, I'm writing a book." He said, "Come on, you can finish it later. What chapter are you on?" I replied, "The one about *Patience*." He said, "Well, you can certainly learn how to be patient while fishing!"

While this may be true, I think I am learning more about patience when I write.

Chinese Ancient Wisdom says, "Patience, patience and more patience is the golden rule". After studying harder, looking closer, and thinking deeper about it, I finally understand what this proverb really means. The first "patience" means "patience is a virtue". The second "patience" is to emphasize the "importance of being patient". And the words "more patience" in the proverb represents the "variety of patience that we need to achieve".

- Patience to endure and persevere.
- Patience to conquer fear and obstacles.
- Patience to hope, plan and achieve.
- Patience to resist temptation and desire.
- Patience to sacrifice and dedicate ourselves.
- Patience to understand and forgive others.

I am lucky to be writing this book. As I am writing, I am learning. We all have innate talent, power, and wisdom; however, we must exercise patience to utilize our abilities in the most effective way. Patience is just like education, it is infinite and endless. I need to get back to basics and try to understand how I can learn patience by fishing.

Eric, I am ready to go fishing!

H.A.P.P.Y.L.I.F.E.

Passion

*If you choose a career
you are passionate about,
you will never work a day in your life.
Find your passion and
live your life in paradise.*

Ancient Wisdom
"Passion is transparency and balance."

Modern Philosophy
*"If you are passionate,
you will not have to work a day in your life."*

Where's My Tip?

I love what I do for a living. I enjoy interacting with my customers in my restaurant. I serve and care for them as though they are my friends. I am happy and satisfied when my customers enjoy their meals. A smile on their faces puts a smile on mine. When I see them returning for another visit, I always appreciate them and feel joyful.

I have enjoyed my business for more than forty years and spend many hours a day in my restaurant. But I have not worked a single day in my life because I have passion for what I do.

I respect my customers and enjoy every conversation I have with them. I once heard the saying, "first-class people have first-class helpers". I consider my customers to be first-class people so I strive to be first-class help to them. I may just be a server, but I want to be the best server I can possibly be. In whatever career you choose, you should strive to be the best, regardless of what you do, or how little or how much money you make.

There once was a father and a son who went into business together. The father shined shoes while the son sold newspapers. Two brothers were frequent customers to their business.

As a common practice, the father shined and polished the older brother's shoes for twenty minutes each time. The younger brother's shoes were being shined for less than five minutes per visit. The younger brother always left a good tip, while the older brother usually left nothing.

H.A.P.P.Y.L.I.F.E.

One day, out of curiosity, the son asked his father why he spent much more time on the older brother's shoes while the younger, good-tipping brother got less of his attention.

The father explained. He said he was there to provide a service and he was passionate about his work. He loved making shoes shiny, a job he considered an art. The older brother always wore old shoes that required the very best skills and techniques to bring out the shine in them. The father said that he always enjoyed the challenge to serve the older brother. On the other hand, the younger brother always wore new shoes and it was easy to make them shine.

I learned a valuable lesson from this story and that's why whenever I serve my customers, their tips are irrelevant. I just want to serve them to the best of my abilities.

There is a Modern Philosophy that teaches us, "What goes around comes around." When we try our best, others will take notice. Their appreciation and the joy of self-satisfaction are our best rewards.

Dad Loved To Cook

My father was a cook for fifty years. I remember when I was younger watching him study cookbooks late at night. As a self-taught chef, he would often cook new recipes for us to try, and they were delicious.

When my father and I were in business together, I was often the one who created new dishes. One of my favorite creations was inspired by President Nixon's visit to China. I developed a nine-course meal called the "Presidential Banquet" that I imagined the President might have eaten on his visit to China.

My dad was the talent behind my creations. I told him my ideas, and he practiced them. It was as if I was the civil engineer designing blueprints and he was the contractor bringing them to fruition. He soon turned several of my ideas into classic dishes.

We gained recognition for innovative entrees and original sauces thanks to my father's passion for cooking. People came from far away to enjoy our creations and delicious meals.

Despite his success, he continued to practice and research cooking techniques. Once he mastered every aspect of an entrée, he started to create unique and beautiful garnishes. He became very skilled in the art of food carving. Eventually, every one of our dishes was also served with a small animal or character garnish carved out of a fruit or a vegetable. If we are passionate about something we do, we will always continue to improve. We will never stop learning and we will achieve great success.

H.A.P.P.Y.L.I.F.E.

My father's job was the same as his hobby – cooking. Even though he spent countless hours at the restaurant cooking, I'm not sure he thought of it as "work." How many people do you know would come home and continue to work for fun? When we are passionate about our job, we will never "work" a day in our lives.

Passionate Politician

Confucius and his students traveled along the Tai-San mountainside. They saw a woman crying on the side of the road. Confucius noticed this and wanted to comfort her.

"Why are you crying?" he asked. She replied, "My husband died last month, he was eaten by a tiger. I was mourning his loss. Last week my son died. A tiger also ate him. Now I am mourning for both of their losses."

Confucius asked, "If you knew a tiger was close to your home, why didn't you and your son move after the first attack?"

"We did not want to move because we love our Governor. He is passionate, honest, fair and cares for the people," she answered.

Confucius expressed his condolences to the lady and turned to his students, "Children, this family did not move for the sake of a good government. We can learn that bad government policies and practices are worse enemies than tigers," he affirmed.

I remember this story from grade school. It was the first piece of Chinese literature I learned. I did not understand its importance, however, until much later in life.

Several years ago, one of my good friends was working as an associate for Mark Warner's campaign for Governor of Virginia. She asked me if I would meet with him because she thought I could provide support and offer my ideas to his campaign. I obliged her request and met with Mr. Warner.

During the meeting, I told Mr. Warner that I was not sure how much help I could offer him, since I was not familiar with his platforms and didn't know if I agreed with them. Mr. Warner looked at me and smiled as he said, "I am open to hearing what you have to say because I am passionate about all Virginians. I just want to make Virginia a better place."

At that moment, the ancient story of the Governor and tiger came flooding back to me. Politicians should be in government to serve the people. As a politician, the best interest of the people should supersede self-enrichment and party line politics. My respect for Mr. Warner grew because of his passion for serving all Virginians. From then on, he had my support.

There's a saying in America that states, "Education is the foundation of mankind". I would extend this message and amend it to, "Education is the foundation of mankind. Government policy is the roof that protects the people"

Teachers are the stewards for better education by sharing their knowledge with our future generations. Politicians should represent the best interests of the people by providing effective policy and passionate leadership to protect our economy and country.

A politician should not be in government because he craves money and power, but because he is passionate about the people he serves.

H.A.P.P.Y.L.I.F.E.

Passionate People Welcome Busy Days

Growing up, one of my childhood friends, Maria, was obsessed with playing the piano. She had started playing when she was five years old and was incredibly talented. In college, she double-majored in nursing and nutrition in hopes of becoming a nutritionist. She knew that a nutritionist had better job prospects and earning potential than a pianist.

Maria now lives in Charlotte, North Carolina and is a piano instructor instead of a nutritionist. She discovered that living your passion is the most prosperous job anyone could ever have.

We've kept in touch throughout the years and it seems that she gets busier as time goes by. Every time I talk to her, I notice that she is always busy teaching her students and organizing piano recitals. Our phone conversations were often very short because of her busy schedule.

Her life is consumed with preparing sheet music, chords and songs for her students. Her weeks are jam-packed with planning and scheduled piano lessons.

When she puts on a recital, she is sleepless with thoughts about its preparation. Many of her students have won trophies in district and regional competitions and she is very proud of them. She loves her job and does not realize how busy she actually is.

Maria completes more work in one day than most people hope to complete in a week. When we are passionate in what we do and are willing to work hard, we are productive. When we are productive, we are rewarded with happiness.

H.A.P.P.Y.L.I.F.E.

A Cook Who Could Paint

About ten years ago, a friend of mine, Yung, called me from New York City and asked me if I had a job for him. I told him of course I did, so he moved here and started working for me.

He was an excellent cook, and I was extremely happy to have him join my restaurant. He prepared good food for our customers and loved to cook for my family and I. We always enjoyed his tasty dishes.

About a month after he started working for me, Yung handed me a painting of a tropical island with a beautiful sunset. He told me that he had painted it for my wife and I as a gift. We happily accepted it. Everyone who saw his painting appreciated his talent and beautiful work.

One day, I asked him why he did not pursue a career as an artist since he had such talent. He told me that he loved to paint and he had been painting since his childhood. He had worked for an art gallery in New York for years, but because he did not have the name recognition in the art world, he was making only a minimum salary.

Yung told me that the high cost of living in New York City finally had caught up with him so he decided to move south and change careers to make a better living.

I am not an artist, but I can appreciate art. I knew that he should not be working for me. He should be pursuing his passion instead.

H.A.P.P.Y.L.I.F.E.

I told him that our restaurant would be a stepping-stone for his future. However, after he saved enough money, he should move back to New York City and try again to become an artist.

Several months later, Yung decided to move back to New York and begin anew. As he was leaving, I knew I would be missing a good friend and a superior chef, but I was happy for him because I knew he would find happiness in painting.

Upon his return to New York City, he began to paint again, selling paintings in Times Square and Central Park for less than $20 apiece. As time progressed, he continued to improve his painting skill and became a popular artist in the area. Soon, he was well regarded and many more clients appreciated his paintings.

Today, Yung is happily making a living selling his own artwork. His paintings now sell for hundreds and up to thousands of dollars. I am a proud owner of several of his beautiful art pieces.

I am fortunate to have made a living doing something I love, serving people. Chasing passion is more rewarding than chasing all the wealth in the world. I encourage my children to find a profession that they will love to do with enthusiasm.

Modern Philosophy states, "The poorest man is the one who has lost his passion in life". If we are not doing something we love, it is never too late to change it and enjoy life.

Toastmasters Don't Burn

There are situations in which transforming your passion into a job is not possible. In that case, it is important to strike a balance. Find a hobby that makes you excited! Go camping, join a book club or learn new games to play with your family (my family plays Chinese Chess!). You could take up gardening, painting or fishing. You could try a new sport such as golf, swimming, or anything else you might enjoy.

After working many years in the restaurant business, I realized that I needed to explore all that life had to offer. Even though I loved what I did for a living, I decided to take some time off for new activities. I discovered new passions that I had no idea I was harboring.

I joined a group called the Toastmasters Club (no, this is not a club for toasting enthusiasts—although I must say I appreciate the electric toaster despite the occasional burnt bread!). This group meets once a week and each meeting has a different theme. Each member prepares a speech, gives an impromptu talk or evaluates other speeches. The Toastmasters Club has helped me develop my speaking, leadership and social skills.

I have also learned an incredible amount of wisdom by listening to my peers speak. I have met many great people in the organization, and I thank them for their support and encouragement. I was inspired as I watched other members improve their speaking abilities by leaps and bounds.

I also found a new passion in writing this book. When I first started brainstorming my thoughts, I was consumed by ideas. Between social and business meetings, I would jot down new ideas. I found myself thinking about this book often; when I went to sleep and when I woke up in the morning. I was excited, enthusiastic and passionate about it. I hope you love reading this book as much as I have loved writing it.

Having a balance in life translates into passion for life. If we are satisfied with what we already have in life, it is easy for us to appreciate and enjoy our jobs too.

Wouldn't it be wonderful if we could improve our productivity and ourselves because we enjoy what we do for a living? When we are happy in our work, we are able to exert half the effort while gaining twice the results. By doing so, the extra energy could improve our productivity and create new opportunities. Soon, we will love our jobs!

Having passion in life is a shortcut to success and happiness.

H.A.P.P.Y.L.I.F.E.

Enjoy Your Own Paradise

Most people believe that paradise is a place that is far away from us and hard to find. Paradise may be wonderful. However, if you do not find something there that makes you happy, it may be a place where you do not want to stay.

When you look closer, and think deeper, you will see that paradise is not far away at all. It is easy to find because happiness is in your state of mind. When you are happy, you are living in paradise.

I have seen many people enjoy life by finding a passion that makes them happy such as reading, painting, playing golf, learning something new or just by talking to others (I am one of those people!). Watching sunrises and sunsets, gazing at the openness of the sky and enjoying the beauty of a mountainside can be fulfilling. Smelling the fragrance of flowers, hearing birds singing, or just resting under the sun can be joyful as well.

When I suffer a great loss or tragedy, I try to understand life and not make things more complicated than they are. Life can be difficult, but this should not prevent us from searching for relief and passion. Life should be enjoyed by all of us even though it seems impossible at times. When we take our time to look closer, we discover the world is beautiful and has more to offer than we imagined possible. Find your passion, and enjoy your own paradise, even if it is only for a short period of time each day.

Relax each day and enjoy a little at a time. You will find that paradise is within you and happiness is easy to attain.

H.A.P.P.Y.L.I.F.E.

Yes

A dream and a plan;
anything is possible.
Yes, we can!

Ancient Wisdom
"The reward goes to the capable."

Modern Philosophy
"Yes, we can!"

H.A.P.P.Y.L.I.F.E.

A Teacher For Life

One of my first teachers in America was a lady named Betty Grigg. She taught me more than simply high school English. She taught me how to believe in myself.

When I first walked into Ms. Grigg's classroom, I quietly found a seat in the back of the room. Realizing I might need help, she moved my seat to the front of the class, next to a helpful student. She asked me to introduce myself to the class. I apologetically told her that I could not speak English. She smiled at me and simply said, "Yes, you can."

Throughout the year, she assigned me helpful homework so I could practice my English. Before each assignment I told her that I couldn't do it. Her reply was always, "Yes, you can."

Thanks to Ms. Grigg's encouragement and teachings, by the end of the year, my English had progressed ten-fold. I knew I could learn the language as long as I had a plan and practiced it.

Turning in my last assignment to Ms. Grigg at the end of the year, I smiled at her and said, "Yes, I can." I guess you can say that we "stole" that motto from President Obama forty years before he actually coined it. Still, the saying is true, "yes, we can".

The following is a letter I received from Betty via her goddaughter:

"I will never forget the way Chin looked when I first saw him, standing at the door of my classroom with the high school counselor. He looked so little, and tried to look so brave when I knew he was bound to be scared standing in front of all the other students for the first time. He had just arrived from Hong Kong.

He took one look at me and bowed from the waist. When the counselor brought him to my desk and introduced him, he bowed again. He was too respectful to look directly at my face. I went to his seat to write down his name, and he stood up so fast that he knocked the desk over. The class laughed. I exploded. I said, 'What if you suddenly found yourself in China? You would have no idea what to do!' I told the class if they laughed at him again or if they didn't help him, I would fail every last one of them!

I admired this poor frightened boy who was so brave and polite. I moved him up to the front row and put the smartest girl in class next to him. I told him to touch her shoulder if he didn't understand something and she would explain it to him, but he never did.

He never took his eyes off me and listened carefully in class. I think I did my best teaching that year, trying to speak slowly and clearly, pausing to make sure he understood.

I went to the teachers meetings and tried to persuade them to pronounce words slower and clearer so Chin could understand what they were saying. When they spoke too fast in their southern accent, it was difficult for him to understand.

He had a hard time that first year, but once he learned what he was supposed to do, he did very well. This was a speech class, and it's difficult for anyone to stand up in front of the class and speak, but even more so if you don't speak English as well as others. I let him do his first speech in Chinese so everyone could see how confident he could be, if given the chance.

H.A.P.P.Y.L.I.F.E.

In one assignment, the students had to demonstrate how to do something. Chin brought a whole chicken and a knife and showed how to cut it up to be cooked in a restaurant. By then, the class wanted to help him instead of make fun of him.

After school, Chin would wait inside my door until the last class was dismissed. He would bring a word he didn't understand or a paper from another class that he wanted me to look at. Even when he was no longer in my class, he came back to me nearly every day with another question. I never saw anyone work harder.

It has been a great pleasure to watch Chin become a successful man. He worked hard and he never gave up. His English became better and better, and soon he was able to enjoy telling stories and even make jokes.

Over the years he has called me and we enjoyed many visits together. He is like one of my sons, and he is the way I would have wanted him to be if he were actually my son. He takes good care of his family. He is a wonderful person, and I do love him dearly. He is the only student I felt that way about."

---- Letter from Betty ----

Betty has been one of the treasures in my life and a wonderful teacher to me for all the years I've known her. She is in her nineties and continues to have a beautiful mind and a warm heart.

Whenever I talk to Betty, it reminds me the value of trust and the importance of believing in ourselves.

Yes, We can! Betty, I love you!

H.A.P.P.Y.L.I.F.E.

Moving Mountains

My mother always encouraged me to help elderly people and young children as much as possible. She told me, "If we help one another, we can move a mountain." I thought to myself, "Move a mountain?" Before I could comment, she told me a story:

There once was an old man who lived in a village. The village was isolated from the rest of the town because of an enormous mountain. The people from the village had to walk several miles around it to get to the market. To help his fellow citizens avoid the long walks, the old man decided he was going to move the mountain.

He started digging. Each day he woke up, took his shovel to the mountain and worked. Each day he came home with an aching back and tired muscles. However, he was determined and never gave up. Rain or shine, he was there early every morning continuing to move the mountain, one shovel at a time.

Many villagers walked past him during his daily digs and asked the old man about what he was doing. When he explained to them about his plan to move the mountain, they laughed as they strolled away.

There was a small and curious boy that lived in the same village as the old man. One day he passed by and saw the old man digging and asked what he was doing. The old man explained, "I am moving the mountain so that our villagers can save hours of traveling time to town."

"Sir, do you think you can do it?" the boy asked excitedly.

"Yes, I can." the old man replied.

Instead of laughing at him, a joyful smile showed up on the boy's face. Without saying a word, he quickly ran back to the village. He returned a short while later with his own shovel, and together the old man and the curious boy worked side by side.

After a day of digging, the boy returned to his friends. He told them about the exciting adventure he had enjoyed while digging with the old man. His story intrigued his friends. The next day they joined the young boy and the old man on their mission. As time went on, the villagers became moved by their enthusiasm and joined in to help.

Months and years went by and they continued to dig tirelessly. Finally, the old man and the boys reached the other side of the mountain. The mountain was never moved, they simply had made a tunnel through it!

My mother had made a point; if the old man can help the villagers to "move a mountain," then we can certainly help our family, friends and others to "move a few bricks".

The old man's vision and determination inspired me to never give up. As long as we are willing to try, anything is possible. "Yes, we can!"

Hope With A Plan, "Yes! We Can!"

We have all heard the motto of "Yes, we can". I have practiced this philosophy all my life. When we believe in ourselves and work hard towards our goal, anything is possible. "Yes, we can!"

I also embrace the message of "hope and change." However, I would amend that message. Hope alone is not enough. We must also have a plan. Hope without a plan is simply a dream, one that often does not come to fruition. Hope with a plan is a vision. When we act on our vision, it becomes a reality.

I have been successful in some of my business ventures because I had vision. When I was seventeen years old, my father and his business partner went to see their loan officer at the Second National Bank in Richmond, Virginia. My father asked me to come to the meeting as a translator because he did not speak English.

During the meeting, I learned that their restaurant was being foreclosed because they had not made principal and interest payments for several months. My father's business partner declined to challenge the foreclosure, but my father wanted to continue the business. He was the chef and had a family to take care of. He needed the job.

My father asked the loan officer if he and I could take over the business and be responsible for the loan payments. The loan officer said, "I don't think so."

H.A.P.P.Y.L.I.F.E.

That sounded like a challenge, and to me, a mission to accomplish. Running out of options, I asked if I could see the President of the bank. I was hoping I could persuade him to allow us to continue the business. The loan officer reluctantly knocked on the President's door. Mr. Norman Robinson came out, pulled up a chair and sat next to me. He asked what he could do for us, and I explained our desire to continue the business.

"How could you make the business work if your father and his partner could not?" Mr. Robinson asked me.

"There are three reasons," I stated. "One, I have already worked in the restaurant at various positions including; manager, dishwasher, cook, cashier, and server, so I understand the business. Two, my father and his partner have families to take care of. They needed their salaries to pay their bills. Since I am single and have no additional expenses, I can work fifteen hours a day, seven days a week during the summer for one dollar per hour to pay the loan. When school starts, I can continue working many hours a week and I can eat free at the restaurant. That will ensure that I can pay the loan on time and in full when it is due."

He looked suspiciously at me and asked, "What is the third reason?"

I scratched my head and looked at him. "I don't have a third reason," I said. We were both silent for a while. Then I finally said, "Because you trust me." He smiled and asked my father and I to come back the next day to sign the loan papers.

H.A.P.P.Y.L.I.F.E.

I became a business owner two months before my eighteenth birthday. Four years later, my father and I paid off the entire note to the bank. It was at that time I found out that my promissory note was void because I had signed it as a minor. Mr. Robinson knew this, but still allowed me to take the loan. He believed in me and trusted that I would not disappoint him.

Though I found myself cornered and out of options, I remained hopeful. By outlining a plan to pay back the loan, I shared my vision with Mr. Robinson. He shared his trust with me, and my dream became a reality.

By having vision, patience, trust and a positive attitude, I was able to position myself to be in the right place at the right time, and was capable of making the right decision. The restaurant was able to continue to be in business.

Yes, I can. Yes! We can!

H.A.P.P.Y.L.I.F.E.

Saying "Yes" To A Stranger

About twenty years ago, my family and I traveled to Hong Kong for a vacation. We were sitting at a hotel enjoying a quiet brunch when my wife suddenly exclaimed, "LOOK! It's Elizabeth Taylor!"

I turned to see three people sitting at a table, clearly in an important business meeting.

"Are you sure she's here in Hong Kong?" I asked my wife.

"Yes, I'm sure! Wouldn't it be wonderful to have her autograph?" Jade replied whimsically.

Having never been afraid to ask for something in the past, I started walking towards the table. While I was walking, I reconsidered my actions. Who did I think I was, interrupting Elizabeth Taylor's meeting for an autograph? Before I could have a second thought about my venture, I was already approaching her table.

"Ms. Taylor, please forgive me for interrupting your meeting," I stammered. "I know you have important business to discuss, but my wife recognized you. She is a big fan of yours and has watched almost every movie you have ever been in. She and I have watched *Cleopatra* six times and we thought you looked so beautiful as the Queen of Egypt in that movie."

She looked at me and turned to my wife and gave her a friendly smile from a distance. I continued, "Do you think I could get your autograph for my wife?"

Ms. Taylor thanked me for our compliments and happily signed her name on the napkin that I handed her.

Half expecting her to shoo me away, I asked for a few more autographs for some of my relatives who were accompanying us. To my surprise, she obliged with grace.

I had no idea what Elizabeth Taylor was going to say to me - a stranger. Lucky for me she ended up being incredibly generous, not only giving me her autograph, but also forgiving my interruption.

Ms. Taylor inspired me to be a humble person. Her charm and gracefulness has lived in our hearts ever since. My wife and I will never be able to thank her enough for her autograph, as well as the kindness she showed me when she said "yes" to a stranger.

We will never know the answer to anything until we ask. We will be surprised how many times "yes" will be the answer and how much we can learn just by asking.

H.A.P.P.Y.L.I.F.E.

Ask Again

I once owned a sports center that was financed by a local bank. Two years later, the business was not profitable and the bank recalled my loan. Financially, I was unable to repay it and was forced to search for a new loan from a different bank.

F & M was the bank I sought for a replacement loan. I drafted a business proposal detailing how I would earn the money to pay back the loan. Upon my request, the loan officer denied me. Desperate, I looked squarely into his eyes and asked if I could re-apply with a new proposal. He told me that he honestly didn't think that a new proposal would change the bank's decision, but I was welcome to re-apply.

After two weeks, I made another appointment with the same loan officer. I presented a completely revamped proposal for my revised application. He was surprised to see me again because he had not expected me to actually re-apply for the loan. "You know, you are the first commercial customer to come back and ask again after being rejected," he said.

"I fully understand, I just don't like to take no for an answer" I replied while I handed him my plan. He looked down at my new proposal and smiled to himself. I'm not sure if my new application was better than the first one or if he just liked my determination. Even though I was denied the first time, the loan officer approved my request when I asked again.

It is easy for someone to say "no" instead of "yes" to others. It is also easy to ask again. Do not miss your opportunity because you are denied the first time. Don't be afraid to ask again!

A "Yes Man" Says "No"

I would consider myself to be a "yes man" as I never like to give "no" for an answer to others. I always tell my friends that I am here for them if they need me. I like to affirm others and am very trusting. I enjoy being with people and tend to surround myself with like-minded individuals.

My friend Eric is also a "yes man". He is one of my closest confidants. He has always said, "Yes" to every favor I have asked of him. I have done the same for him.

When I first told Eric about my plan to write this book, he was extremely excited about my idea. But when I asked him to help me to write it, to my surprise, his answer was, "No!"

"It is your book and if you want it bad enough, I know you will do it on your own" he said to me. "I would rather read your book than help you write it."

His "no" was encouragement for me to start writing. Eric knew I could do it by myself. If not, I would be able to find a way to achieve my goal.

There are many ways to get to Rome. All we need to do is decide if we really want to go there. Modern Philosophy tells us "if there's a will, there's a way".

Sometimes a "no" is really a "yes" in disguise. When you want to achieve your goal, you need to say, "yes" to yourself. View denial as a new opportunity, knowing "yes, you can!"

H.A.P.P.Y.L.I.F.E.

The Value Of Yes

When Ms. Grigg and Mr. Robinson told me, "Yes, you can" they were really telling me that they trusted me. Ms. Grigg trusted my abilities. When I finally realized that "yes, I could", I began to trust in my abilities too. Mr. Robinson trusted my vision when he said "yes" to my loan request. The value of yes is trust.

If we trust people, transactions will move much faster. I handle money and make change in my restaurant every day. When someone gives me a large amount of coins, it is much faster to trust that it is the correct amount instead of counting out each and every penny.

When I was in my early thirties, I decided to pursue a business in commercial real estate. In order to start this endeavor, I needed to take out a loan.

I made an appointment with Dominion Bank Executive Vice President, Mr. Wellford Maxie, to propose my business plan. During our conversation, I wanted to convince him that I was someone he could trust. I began to tell him the story of my relationship with my previous banker, Mr. Robinson, and how he trusted me after our first meeting. Before I could finish, Mr. Maxie said, "I've heard your story. I have worked with Mr. Robinson before, and he told me all about you."

I laughed and asked him, "So you trust me?" He said, "You come back tomorrow and we'll have the paperwork ready for you." It was a short and productive meeting, to say the least.

In order to be trusted, however, we have to gain respect by practicing what we preach. I told Mr. Maxie that he could trust me to pay the loan payments every month on time, and I was determined not to disappoint him.

One of my loan payments was due on a day that the city experienced a horrible snowstorm. I called Mr. Maxie to tell him I was on my way to deliver my payment. To my surprise, he told me the bank was closing at noon because of the weather conditions. Determined, I told him I would be there anyway. The usual fifteen-minute drive took me one-and-a-half hours but Mr. Maxie waited for me.

Even though I had trouble getting to the bank due to icy roads, I had kept my word and made my payment on time.

Saying "yes" and trusting people are effective relationship building tools. I did not learn how important this was until fifteen years ago. In managing my restaurants and other businesses, I was a one-man army and always made all of my managerial decisions myself.

This practice became incredibly overwhelming once I started investing in commercial real estate. So I started to share the responsibility with my managers. In doing so, I gained more time and energy to spend with my family and my other business ventures. My businesses became more productive and profitable, and my relationships with my managers became solid friendships. As it turned out, my family and friends appreciated me more because I had more time to spend with them. I became a happier person, as well.

We can imagine that if we all worked to say "yes" more often in our daily lives. We would be friendlier and a lot happier. We can also improve our efficiency and productivity as long as we have a plan and trust in ourselves.

When I was writing this book, I often had to remind myself, "Yes, I can!" Otherwise, I would have doubted my abilities and never accomplished my goal.

Practicing what we preach will break down barriers and yield success. By saying, "Yes I can!" along with hoping, planning and trusting others and ourselves, we all can achieve our goals and attain happiness.

"Yes, we can!"

H.A.P.P.Y.L.I.F.E.

Love

Love is caring, educating and sharing openly and unconditionally, without boundaries.

Ancient Wisdom
*"Love is priceless,
the strongest tie among men."*

Modern Philosophy
"Love like it is your last day."

H.A.P.P.Y.L.I.F.E.

My Love Story

Growing up in Hong Kong meant sharing an apartment with several other families. One of the families that shared our apartment was a girl named Jade and her aunt. When I was a young boy I adored Jade, but I was too young to really understand what love really meant. After a few years, Jade's family moved out of our apartment. Even though I did not see her again until several years later, I never forgot her.

A few months before I moved to America, I attended my cousin's wedding shower. Because I had school, I was late to the lunch. My family saved me some food and I ate by myself in the kitchen. As I started to eat, a beautiful young girl joined me at the table.

I recognized her at once. It was Jade, the girl I had known all those years ago! She was also late to the shower, and we enjoyed a private lunch while the ceremony continued in the next room. We both were very shy, so it was a quiet lunch. Still, I couldn't forget about that time with her, and I knew I had to see Jade again before I moved to the U.S.

A few days before I left Hong Kong for America, I suggested to my mother that we visit Jade's apartment to say goodbye to her and her aunt. When we got there, I didn't see Jade anywhere, and was devastated. I asked her aunt, "Where is Jade?" She said Jade was in the shower and would be out soon. My heart leapt. Soon, she entered the room, and she looked gorgeous. She was very thankful for our visit and so was I.

We didn't stay long at Jade's home, for we had other goodbyes to say. As we were leaving, I turned my head to look at her one last time. We caught each other's eyes. I left elated and love-struck.

On the airplane trip to the U.S., I asked my mother about what she thought of Jade. She said that Jade was a fantastic girl who was sweet, hard working, and had a big heart. She liked Jade a lot. Without admitting it, I implied that she was my dream girl. My mother agreed.

After I came to America, I found myself consumed with school, hard work and long hours at the restaurant. Life was difficult at times.

Still, I never forgot about Jade. Long distance phone calls were costly and, therefore, out of the question, so I started writing. I sent cards and letters whenever I could. I always waited anxiously for a reply from Jade, and whenever I received a letter from her, my heart skipped a beat.

Because I worked long hours at the restaurant, I did not have much time for a social life. Her caring letters became my only companions among the endless hours of work and school. I checked my mail every day.

When I was nineteen years old, I was drafted to serve the U.S. Army in Vietnam. I wrote Jade a letter telling her I might be going to war. She wrote back, showing an incredible amount of compassion. Jade told me she loved me and asked me to be careful while I was serving my country. Her love encouraged me to devote myself to my country. I told Jade I loved her too and our relationship escalated.

H.A.P.P.Y.L.I.F.E.

I never went to Vietnam, as my case was deferred because the war was winding down. Still, I had already planned time off at the restaurant. I figured since I had my affairs together, I should take the opportunity to go to Hong Kong to visit Jade instead.

I told Jade I was thinking about coming to visit her. We were both very excited about the idea, as we had not seen each other in four years.

I asked my parents if I could go to Hong Kong to visit Jade. My mother asked me if I loved Jade enough to pay the expensive plane ticket to see her. I told my mother that I had fallen in love with Jade and I needed to see her. My mother said, "Well, if that is the case, are you going home to marry her?"

I replied joyfully, "That is beyond my wildest hopes and dreams. I would love to have her as my wife." Immediately, I wrote Jade a letter and asked her if she would marry me. I didn't know what to expect in her reply. Waiting for her letter seemed like an eternity.

Finally, I received her reply. My hands were shaking and my heart was racing as I removed the letter from the mailbox. I nervously tore the envelope open.

She told me she felt drunk after she read my letter even though she had never drank a glass of wine in her life. She happily said, "Yes!"

I went back to Hong Kong that summer and married Jade. She was beautiful and kind, and had the warmest heart I had ever known. Our wedding day was the happiest day of my life.

H.A.P.P.Y.L.I.F.E.

Shortly after our wedding day, I had to leave my wife to come back to America and resume my busy schedule. A year later, Jade received her immigration visa approval and she came to the United States to join me.

In love, you must practice patience. I certainly learned this while waiting to see Jade and be reunited with her after we got married. Because I loved her, I waited, hoping and yearning for the time we could see each other again.

I sacrificed my time and learned how to be patient while I was waiting for Jade. I endured many sleepless nights thinking and worrying about her well-being. Once we were together, each moment became precious. In return, we both shared unequivocal happiness.

One thing Jade loves about me is that I never complain when I am at home (Of course I don't. She's the one who does most of the housework! Thank You Jade!)

After many years of marriage, our love and commitment to each other has remained steadfast. We cheer each other on in the good times and offer our support to each other during bad times.

Enjoying your family is extremely important in life. Value your relationship with your loved ones. Take care of each other with sincerity and a loving mind.

Share your love with passion, patience and sacrifice. When you are willing to give your love without conditions, the joy of love will flow back to you in a stream of happiness.

H.A.P.P.Y.L.I.F.E.

The Man I Grew To Respect And Love

My relationship with my banker, Mr. Robinson, eventually developed into a lasting friendship. He would often frequent my restaurant for lunch. I always knew exactly what he wanted—wonton soup and chicken chow mein. He would stay and talk with me, and we became friends. We began to talk business and he taught me the ropes of the commercial real estate industry. He would often invite me to go with him to look at new developments, and taught me how to evaluate the potential of business properties. I have learned so much from his teachings and wisdom.

During the car rides to visit various properties, we truly connected with each other. He became a father figure to me, and I respected him for all of his advice and friendship. Our relationship grew as time went on.

Unfortunately, a few years after Mr. Robinson and I first met, he had a heart attack. He was hospitalized for seventeen days. I visited him daily between my classes and my shifts at the restaurant. Every day I would bring him his lunch. I fed him, helped him with his exercises and kept him company.

During those visits, our bond became even tighter. Our families became close, and my wife and I were often invited for dinner at Mr. Robinson's home. He came to the restaurant to see us several times a week. We cared for each other like family.

One Thanksgiving holiday, my wife Jade and I were invited to join Mr. Robinson and his family for dinner. It was a cold, chilly, drizzling evening so I wore a long raincoat to attend the dinner party.

When we were inside of Mr. Robinson's home, he assisted me with taking off my coat. My manners told me I should not receive this honor since he was my mentor and I was his junior. I reluctantly accepted.

We had a wonderful dinner and a great time together. As we were leaving, Mr. Robinson insisted to put my coat back on for me. Once again, I humbly accepted his kindness with gratitude and appreciation.

I felt his love when Mr. Robinson was putting my coat on for me. When I think about that moment, my blood always flows and tears come to my eyes. If you are one of my family members, friends or customers, (regardless of your age) it is always my honor to put your coat back on for you. Mr. Robinson taught me that love and kindness has no boundaries.

I came to love Mr. Robinson. A few years after the first heart attack, he had a second, and then a third heart attack. I went to visit him daily during each hospitalization. During one visit, he held my hand and told me how he thought of me as a son. Tears were in our eyes. I wanted to tell him how much I loved him, but I held back my feelings. He died a few days later.

I regret that I did not share my thoughts and feelings with Mr. Robinson. I wish I had told him how highly I regarded him and how much I loved him. Years later, I learned a Western Philosophy proverb that says, "Love your loved ones like it is your last day." I wish I had learned it sooner.

I have met some famous and highly revered people in this world, but none of them compare to Mr. Robinson. Because of his love and trust, he is the most famous man in my life. He will always live in my heart. Love truly has no boundaries.

H.A.P.P.Y.L.I.F.E.

Five People On A Honeymoon

When we got married, Jade and I had little money and we were not able to go on a honeymoon. Years later, we went to Disney World as our belated honeymoon. However, instead of just the two of us, we brought along our three children.

Our driving trip to Disney was almost as fun as our excursions to the parks. My kids may disagree with me, but I think my favorite part of the trip was during the drive down to Florida. For the entire trip there were a lot of exciting moments. We talked about everything from UFOs and aliens to school, education and relationships. We encouraged each other's creativity by sharing stories, riddles, and jokes. I could say we laughed all the way to the park.

That trip proved to us that our family was very close. One would think that a fourteen-hour car ride would end in siblings fighting and parents not speaking to each other, but this was not the case. I almost didn't want to get out of the car when we arrived because I was having such a good time, although I'm sure my children were very anxious to get out and explore!

We love being with our children. Any time that we are with them is cherished. Wherever we travel, we always take them with us. To me, quality time with my family is more important than the number of people on a honeymoon.

On the way back to Virginia, one of my children asked us when we were going on our next honeymoon! I told my children, "As long as I am with my family, every day is a honeymoon to me."

Aurea

One of my friends is very wealthy. One day he came to me miserable. He thought his children only called him when they needed his financial assistance. He told me that I had become one of his best friends because I never asked him for anything; instead I always gave him advice and support.

I told him that I may be his best friend, but I would never be a replacement for his children. We need our children. I asked him about the times when he was a young father, changing his children's diapers and toting them to baseball games, and whether he expected them to return the love he extended. He said he had never thought about it that way.

I asked him why he started calculating their love now. I suggested to him that he should tell the children how much he loved them, and to continue to love them the way he always had, instead of expecting something in return.

Tears streamed down my friend's face. He knew I was right. Because of our conversation, he remembered that the value of love is much more than money. Months later, I knew that he and his children were spending more time together and enjoying each other's company.

I learned this lesson for myself when my daughter and I went into business together. Yee May has always loved fashion and shopping. I wanted to help her create a business with this passion, so I helped her open her own jewelry store

H.A.P.P.Y.L.I.F.E.

I invested my time and energy in the business, as well as my life savings, out of love for my daughter. Together, we created a beautiful store that sold stunning works of art, jewelry and collectibles. We named it "Aurea".

My wife, our daughter Yee May and I spent many weeks collectively designing the interior of the store. We traveled to Las Vegas, Atlantic City, New York City, Atlanta and many other places to attend jewelry shows together. We picked out the very best pieces to sell in our stores. Through these joyful journeys, we became even closer. We strengthened our love with our shared interest in Aurea.

However, due to the downturn in the economy, the business did not stay afloat and we had to close the store. I lost a lot of money, but I would do it again if given the choice.

A friend of mine felt sorry for my venture. I told him not to feel that way. I told him that it takes a lot of courage to be in business and it takes even more to accept the consequences. The fact that our family and I learned how to deal with our loss while remaining hopeful and continuing to be happy is amazing.

Even though our business did not work out, I am grateful for the experience. I was given this precious opportunity to spend time with my wife and daughter and share my love while trying to help our daughter cultivate her passions. I would not trade any of this for anything.

When I Was Sick

I was diagnosed with prostate cancer a few years ago. Fortunately for me, it was caught in the early stages. I underwent surgery and when I woke up in the recovery room, my wife was holding my hand and my children were surrounding me. Their love, presence and concern eased the pain.

True love certainly shows its face in hard times. During my six-week recovery, my wife did not rest until I was asleep. She gave up her own daily life to wait on me hand and foot. Staying home, instead of working at the restaurant, she helped me walk and exercise. She supported me, arm in arm, as I took my first steps after the surgery. She helped me dress, bathe and changed my catheters and dressings. If that's not love, I don't know what else is.

Jade even cooked every meal for me, something that rarely happens, as we usually eat at the restaurant. I was lucky enough to enjoy her fine cooking for an entire month-and-a-half. I truly believe that the dishes she cooked, prepared with love and patience, helped me get well. If it were not for her love and compassion, I think I would still be in bed recovering.

Taking care of someone in need is one of the best ways to show and share our love. In addition, it is extraordinarily rewarding. Through her care, cooking and assistance, Jade showed more love for me than I ever imagined possible. When she did, I fell even more deeply in love with her.

We find love by sharing love.

H.A.P.P.Y.L.I.F.E.

A Midnight Meal

In order for us to love someone fully, it is important to learn and understand the ones we love. My father-in-law suffered a stroke many years ago and had lived with us for over twenty years. Several years ago, my family awoke to the banging of pots and pans at three o'clock in the morning. My father-in-law was preparing a dinner for himself.

We tried to stop him, explaining that he had already eaten dinner and did not need to eat again until morning. He resisted, so I prepared a more breakfast-like meal for him, a banana, cereal and milk. He again refused and became emotional, saying that he needed to eat his dinner.

Then, I took him to the window and showed him that it was dark outside. I attempted to explain that it was the middle of the night. He started shouting and fighting. I started getting frustrated. He yelled and claimed that we didn't love him. I definitely disagreed with that, so I yelled back.

Ultimately, we both settled down and everyone went back to sleep. The next morning, he woke up and acted as if nothing had happened the previous night. We assumed he was sleepwalking and did not give this event any further attention.

Later that week, we found him standing, fully clothed, inside of the bathtub. He was hitting the walls with his fists. We asked him what he was doing. He told us he was playing Kung Fu and refused to stop.
I embraced him, pulling his body away from the wall and bathtub.

My wife and I realized that something might be seriously wrong with our father. We sought medical attention for him and he was diagnosed with Alzheimer's disease.

I regret the way I yelled at my father-in-law. Once I understood his diagnosis, my love, adoration and admiration grew for him. I learned to love and care for him more sensitively. The medications that the doctor had prescribed to my father-in-law were able to help him. He lived happily, with our love, for many more years.

I had learned a very important lesson with my father-in-law. Before we lose our temper with the ones we love, we must strive to understand the reasons behind their thinking and behavior. If we don't, we are running the risk of hurting not only our loved one's feelings, but also our own.

H.A.P.P.Y.L.I.F.E.

The Ways We Love

When we love someone, we should always strive to improve our relationship with him or her. We need to support and embrace our loved ones in both hardship and joy.

I know our children love my wife and myself very much. I know this because of the ways they show and share their love.

Our youngest son Ken shows his love with his actions. As a child, he would come into our bedroom every morning before he left for school and give us each a kiss on the cheek. During the winter, he always tugged blankets over our cold feet. He was, and is, an attentive and caring individual and he loves to help others.

My daughter Yee May illustrates her love with her thoughtfulness. She always shows her happy face with a broad smile when she sees my wife and I. She also brings our favorite treats or other small presents when she visits us, even when there is no special occasion. She is always upbeat and has the unique ability to brighten the day of those around her, especially us, her parents.

My son John demonstrates his love through his respect. All of his life, he has never talked back to his parents. He is always polite, patient and content in life. I am proud to say that he is a happy man.

Though in very different ways, my children have showed me more love than I could have ever expected.

I understand that there are some families that have not seen each other or spoken with their loved ones for a while. It is easy to change that. If you have not seen your family lately, pick up the phone and ask them how they are doing or go visit them, if you can.

Sometimes family members are not on speaking terms. Most of the time this is due to minor misunderstandings that become long-lasting conflicts. We continue the hurtful feelings out of stubbornness and an unwillingness to forgive. We will never regain the moments that we miss with our loved ones.

Chinese Ancient Wisdom advises us, "step back one step; the ocean will get wider and the sky broader." Taking a step away from the situation will help us see it more clearly. With forgiveness in mind, we can find a reason to improve our family's relationships with each other and enjoy love.

I would not trade the love I share with my family and friends for any amount of money. After losing both my mother and father, I know the importance of sharing my love with those around me, as one does not know how many more opportunities we have to do so. We should love our loved ones as if it is our last day.

Cherish, enjoy and remember your loved ones. When we experience love, we understand what happiness is really about. It is difficult to be unhappy when we are in love.

H.A.P.P.Y.L.I.F.E.

Improvement

*Improve one step each time and improve
one percent each day
toward your goal and perfection.*

Ancient Wisdom
*"Unless you keep moving forward,
the tide will push you backward."*

Modern Philosophy
"Try, try and try again."

A Penny A Day

When I was a child, my mother always asked me to save my coins in a jar. I had little money, but I was asked to save at least one coin per day. For years I did not understand this request, but I did what my mother told me to do.

I soon noticed that I had no money to spend because the few coins I did have were being deposited in the jar. I finally asked my mother why she was asking me to save these coins when they were so few.

She told me that in saving my coins, I was learning patience. I continued to save. After a year and a half, the jar was heavy. I showed it to my mother.

"You see? One coin may seem unimportant, but the jar became full over time," she said. "You have improved yourself by improving a little each day."

We should strive to improve ourselves one percent towards perfection each day. Think of it like saving a penny. It is only one percent of a dollar, but over time you will reach a nice amount.

The principles I am outlining in this book are intended to help us improve our lives and find happiness. Theoretical knowledge of these principles is important, but this knowledge is useless unless we can apply it in a practical fashion. Ancient Wisdom says, "unless we keep moving forward, the tide will push us backward."

I have found that implementing these virtues in our lives may be difficult at times, but Modern Philosophy says, "if at first we don't succeed, try, try, try again." If we want to be happier, we must strive to improve ourselves. Even it is just a little at a time.

Spear Versus Shield

There once was a King who ordered all of the weapon makers in his kingdom to report to his palace. The King asked each of the craftsmen to produce the sharpest spear and strongest shield they could and bring them back to him in six months.

The craftsmen returned with their spears and shields as requested by the King. All the weapons were crafted in many different forms and styles. The King ordered for each spear to hit each shield so that he could determine the best weapon. In the end, the same craftsman had made both the sharpest spear and strongest shield.

The King asked, "Which one is better, the spear or the shield?"

No one could answer. The room grew silent.

"You must make me something to penetrate the shield," the King said decidedly to the best weapon smith.

"This will be a difficult task, your Majesty," said the weapon maker. "I produced the strongest shield for you."

"I want a better spear to attack the enemy in case they have a shield like mine," replied the King.

"It will take at least two years, but I will do my best," the craftsman said. Reluctantly, the King agreed to this condition.

The weapon maker toiled day and night. Finally, he produced a spear sharp enough to penetrate his strongest shield. He sent it to the King who was pleased with the craftsmanship, but was not satisfied.

"Now you must produce a shield to stop the spear you just made," said the King.

"Yes, my King, but it will take me several years because I must go search for stronger material," replied the craftsman.

The King agreed to the longer deadline and waited. The weapon maker returned to the palace with an impenetrable shield.

The King was extremely happy. "This is wonderful, but now it is your duty to make me a spear that can penetrate this shield," he said.

The smith accepted this new assignment without complaint and said, "Your Highness, thank you for your request. Your command drove my desire to improve. Without your order, I would never have strived to make my weapons that much better. As the task got harder, my skill continued to get better and my confidence rose to meet the challenges as the standards got higher."

Sometimes we need a little push from others to motivate us to improve. When someone demands the best out of us, we must welcome the new challenge as an opportunity to advance our diligence and our skills.

H.A.P.P.Y.L.I.F.E.

Being A Team Player

Improving oneself also improves the lives of others. When you are improving, it motivates others around you to do the same. As a junior in a local high school, I joined the soccer team. I had enjoyed playing soccer in Hong Kong ever since I was eight years old.

During one game the coach yelled from the sidelines, "Pass it! Pass it! Chin, pass it!" Reluctantly, I passed the ball to my closest teammate. As I had expected, he lost control of the ball immediately and forfeited it to the other team.

I said to myself, "If I could have kept the ball a little longer, and carried it forward a little further, we could have had a better chance to score!"

After the game was over, my coach approached me and said, "I know that you are a more experienced and skilled player, but the game of soccer is new to the other students. In order for us to improve, you must help your teammates and pass them the ball during practice and games." I listened to my coach's advice. I began to improve my passing skill. I started looking for open teammates and sending them the ball accurately. We improved our skills and teamwork.

Soon the season came to a close. During our last game, the whole team worked together and we played very hard. Our performance was at its peak and we played our best game of the season.

After the game, our coach was energetic and pleased with our performance. He knew that we had gone from playing as individuals to playing as a team. He told us that he was so proud of us. I had improved myself by helping to improve my teammates.

Don't Miss The Handle

Everyone has heard the expression, "every little bit counts." I firmly believe this. Just as pennies add up to larger amounts, small details make a big difference.

I kept this in mind when I was planning for my restaurants. I added various types of plants to perk up the dining areas. Chinese vases and trinkets are displayed at the entrance of the restaurant for customers to admire and purchase. My favorite addition to my restaurants though, is the trash receptacle handle that I designed.

I noticed whenever customers threw away their leftovers they usually push the container door open with their trays. This caused the food to get on the container or on their clothes. To prevent this from happening to my customers, I personally designed a new handle. This way, my customers can easily push the receptacle door open with their hand and cleanly put away their trash. If you ever come to visit my restaurant, don't miss the handle!

True, a trash receptacle handle may not make or break my customers' experience at the restaurant, and some customers might not even notice the difference, but if the handle can prevent one customer from spilling something, it is worth it. It is the little things that count.

If each one of us can improve a little, for others and for ourselves, these small things will cause a rippling effect that will benefit our communities and better our lives for many years to come.

Mission Accomplished

You may be thinking that you are too young or too old to achieve some of your goals. I don't see it that way. It is never too early, or too late to try to improve yourself and your situation in life.

My aunt moved from Hong Kong to California when she was 63 years old to join her son, leaving her 83 year-old mother behind. (The same person that received resuscitation from her grandson many years earlier} Since my great-aunt was unable to receive a visa to come to this country along with her daughter, it was an extremely difficult choice for my aunt to leave her mother alone in Hong Kong.

My aunt asked me if I could help her mother to obtain a traveling visa so she could join them in America. We were successful and her mother was able to visit the family.

My great-aunt enjoyed American life so much that she wanted to stay in America and become a legal immigrant. This proved to be more difficult as her birth certificate and school records had been lost during World War II. Her application had been denied many times by the Immigration and Naturalization Service. Wanting to help, I testified on her behalf, assisted her in providing pictures, letters and other documents of verification.

Several months later, my great-aunt was requested by the Immigration Department to have an interview with one of the officers.

On that appointment day, I accompanied my great-aunt as a translator. Her family came along to show their support. The drive to the meeting was filled with excitement and nervousness.

During the interview, the immigration officer asked my great-aunt why she wanted to be a legal immigrant. She said, "America is now my home. I have no other place to go and have enjoyed living here these past years. When I die, I want to rest here forever, legally." The officer then asked how old she was.

With a proud smile she replied, "Ninety-five years old." With that, the officer politely asked us to wait and that he would be back in a little while. Shortly thereafter, he returned. "Congratulations, you are now a legal immigrant," the officer said to my great-aunt as he handed a green card to her. Along with a broad smile, he then handed her another document and said, "Here is your Social Security card, now you can start looking for a job!"

Tears running out of our eyes (partly from the laughter at the thought that anyone would hire my great-aunt, at ninety-five years old, for work). We shook hands with the officer and thanked him for his help. We hugged and celebrated with each other for my great-aunt's good fortune.

It is never too early, or too late to fulfill our dreams. Dreams can be small or they can be large. Take initiative and create your own opportunity to make your dreams come true.

If we plan for our dreams, anything can be accomplished. When your dreams come true, you will find plenty of smiles and happiness.

H.A.P.P.Y.L.I.F.E.

Plan Your Work And Work Your Plan

Thomas Edison said, "Genius is one-percent inspiration and ninety-nine percent perspiration." Ancient Wisdom says, "Accomplishment is the combination of preparation and determination." Those philosophies teach me that if I just work hard but without a plan, I would possibly be wasting my energy or just be going around in a circle. If I plan for my work but don't work hard, I probably won't be able to move forward or might even lose ground. To be successful, we must plan our work and work our plan.

One summer day when I was a teenager, I was playing soccer with a friend in his backyard. We were having a great time, running, kicking, and joking with each other. My friend told me that his neighbor had been acting strangely. He has been working in his garage all day long for months and was too busy to even say "hello" to his neighbors.

My friend was curious to find out what his neighbor was doing in the garage. I said, "I can help you find out." He asked me, "How?" Instead of answering him, I just kicked the soccer ball over the fence. "Are you crazy? What are you doing?" my friend cried out. I said, "I'm going to your neighbor's yard and find out what is going on in that garage."

I approached the neighbor's front door. There was no answer, so I walked over to the garage and knocked. An elderly gentleman came out and sternly said, "What are you doing here?" I said, "I came to apologize to you because we kicked our ball into your yard. I didn't want to be impolite by getting my ball without you knowing it."

He said, "That's perfectly alright, just get your ball and leave." I said, "Sir, I play with my friend next door all the time and he noticed that you are always working in your garage." The man said, "Yes, I have been working on a big project in there." I said, "Wow, how big is your project?" He said, "For me, this project is pretty big, because I work alone. I have been planning and working on it for a while now. I will complete it in the next couple of months."

"To be honest with you, Sir, we kicked the ball into your yard out of curiosity, to find out what you were doing in your garage. I hope you forgive both of us." I said, as I pointed to my friend. The old man's stern face turned soft, and he said to me with a friendly smile, "When I was young, I was curious too. That is why I got involved with so many different projects." He opened the door and invited my friend and I into his garage. Once we entered, he closed the door and turned off the lights.

At first, we both were scared but suddenly we realized what he had been doing. He said, "Boys, we are in the Milky Way galaxy. This is what it looks like from Earth." Our mouths hung open, and both of us were thinking "Wow". We looked around the garage in awe. We could not believe what we were seeing. There were stars and planets hanging everywhere, of all shapes, sizes and colors.

He walked to a spot and said, "This is Earth, boys. We are here." He continued to illustrate our solar system and explained how gravity works.

We both were excited. My friend said, "No wonder you were too busy to talk to me lately! Are you doing this for the school or the government?"

The neighbor laughed and said, "I am good, but not that good. No, I'm not building this model for the school or government. Ever since I was a young boy, I wanted to build a galaxy model. It has always been my passion, but it just took me much longer to get started than I had expected."

We were too young to really understand the galaxy, but we were amazed and overwhelmed by it. We admired his achievement. I asked, "How did you know how to build this universe?"

He replied, "I've studied the galaxy for decades. I told my friends and colleagues that I wanted to utilize my knowledge to build a galaxy model with my own hands. They laughed and told me it was a waste of effort." He continued, "I had been planning this project for many years before I put the first nail into the wall. One might say that I planned my work and I worked my plan."

We admired this elderly gentleman but we never really understood what he meant by "plan your work and work your plan."

My life experiences have always unfolded in a last-minute, impromptu and down-to-the-wire fashion. Because of that lack of planning, I have made plenty of mistakes.

When I started writing this book, I soon realized how little I knew and how much more I needed to learn. I soon fully grasped the wisdom of "planning my work and working my plan" and learned how to improve myself in the process. When we have a dream, plan first, and then practice that plan. If we fail, we need to try again, and again and again. When we have a plan, we can make our plan work!

H.A.P.P.Y.L.I.F.E.

Make Your Own Key

Ancient Wisdom teaches us "in order to conquer your obstacles, you must sharpen your tools." Improving your skills helps to rebuild and improve your life. Improving your attitude helps you turn negative experiences into positive outcomes. Transforming weaknesses into strengths will help you discover happiness.

A few years ago, I experienced one tragedy after another. I lost many business deals and, subsequently, lost a lot of money. I also was diagnosed with cancer and underwent surgery. Instead of giving up when I was bruised and battered, I kept moving. I found new passions in life. By not working as much, I could spend more time with my family and enjoy our love. I found value in life because I was able to reconstruct my goals to continue living happily.

Continuing to better yourself helps you to develop the courage and confidence to achieve the new goals you set for yourself. Take the writing of this book for example, the concept started as a lecture that I gave to high school students.

After reading the students' reviews of my lecture, I realized that I wanted to spread my message further. I gained the courage to start writing this book. With the help of several family members and friends, my ideas became better and better. Each day we worked on this project, our ideas, stories and organization improved. I am now confident that I can achieve any of my goals.

I once employed a young woman who improved her life significantly by simply working hard to achieve her goal. I met Betsy when she was sixteen years old. She came into my restaurant one day and asked for a job. I told her she was too young to work at my restaurant. With desperation in her eyes, she told me about her family. She did not have a father or mother and was living with her aunt. No longer wanting to be a financial burden to her aunt, she decided to work and make money to help her aunt and support herself.

I decided to hire her for weekend shifts. Because she did not have any money, I paid for her uniform out of my own pocket. She turned out to be a great employee. She learned very quickly and was incredibly attentive to customers. She eventually graduated from high school and earned enough money to support herself. Through determination and hard work she improved her financial situation and put herself on the path to a happy life.

When we improve ourselves, we also create new opportunities. Betsy improved her financial situation and was able to move out of her aunt's house and start a new life. My high school soccer team improved, and the following year was able to compete in the playoffs. The Vietnamese refugee who taught me Chinese Chess improved his English and was able to start his own business in Philadelphia.

Applying for a job is a great opportunity to improve our circumstances in life. We may have lost our jobs recently, and we may be having a hard time finding new employment, but it's incredibly important to be able to improve and market ourselves appropriately to potential employers.

When you apply for a job, you must have the same mindset as if you are doing the hiring. Ask yourself these questions:

Why do I want to work for this company?

What can I contribute to this company?

What are my strengths and how can I utilize them?

What are my weaknesses and how can I turn them into strengths?

How can I continue to improve others and myself at work?

Does this job have growth potential?

What does success and failure mean to me?

How can I achieve my goals?

Am I qualified and ready for the job?

Why should I be hired?

After you answer these questions, do you think you would hire yourself? If not, improve! The key to success rests in your own hands. Create the key that works for you. When we can improve one step each time and improve one percent each day towards our goal and perfection, we will be successful and we can find happiness in life.

We all can create our own keys unlock our full potential.

H.A.P.P.Y.L.I.F.E.

Fairness

*Life may not be fair to you,
but you must be fair in life.*

Ancient Wisdom
*We need to treat others the way
that we want to be treated."*

Modern Philosophy
*"Unless we are fair to ourselves,
we can never be fair to others."*

A Tough Negotiator

As a businessman, I understand the importance of knowing how to negotiate. I have come to realize that the power of negotiating is not in what you say, but how you say it. You must also have a handle on the issues and understand the type of person with whom you are negotiating.

We must be aware that good negotiation skills and tactics can lead to a position where you find yourself taking advantage of others. The good deal you struck may be sweet now, but guilt is a bitter and lingering taste.

I hired one of my friends as my lawyer when I was involved in an important business transaction. I asked him if he could possibly charge me less.

Being a friend, he said that he was already charging me as little as he could. He said the work that I asked him to perform was time-consuming and difficult. I thought about it and offered him a deal, free lunch and dinner for a lower fee from him. He accepted.

His work turned out to be invaluable. After several profitable years, I began to have second thoughts about underpaying him for his incredible service.

Despite my guilty feeling, I did not learn my lesson the first time. When I redesigned one of my restaurants, I wanted it to be adorned with beautiful paintings and intricate woodwork.

I hired a carpenter to fashion a Chinese-inspired entranceway, as well as other arches throughout the restaurant. Trying to make the best deal possible, I negotiated hard with him. At first, he wanted to refuse my proposal, but I reminded him that he needed my business. He reluctantly accepted my offer. He did beautiful work and performed with his heart and soul. The job took him several months instead of several weeks to complete.

After he finished, I praised his skill and performance. Based on the amount of time he worked, I ended up paying him less than minimum wage per hour. I also discovered that his wife was out of work and he had to support many children with the measly salary I paid him. I did not feel good about the position that I had put him in. I wrote him another check. It seemed like the fair thing to do.

I learned from these experiences. I will never take advantage of the services of others again. I have learned not to squeeze the lemon too dry and always leave some juice for the next person.

A smart and tough negotiator is not the one who just talks tough or acts tough. When we are negotiating, we have a mission to create a "win-win" situation for all parties involved. Ancient Wisdom taught us, "What goes around, comes around". It is true that unless it is a good deal for all, it is never a good deal.

Burdensome Emotions

My mother always told me that jealousy, greed and hatred are always a burden on our shoulders and we must rid ourselves of them so that we can truly be happy.

A few years ago, several friends and I founded a bank. Our group consisted of successful business owners, fundraisers, former bank executives and a judge. We organized the operation and served the bank as the Board of Directors. Everything seemed to be going great. We hired additional bank employees as well as a bank President.

One of our hired employees eventually became a member of the Board. Soon after, he sought more power and more decision-making authority. A month later he recommended re-electing a new Board of Directors as a formality.

As soon as we agreed on this, he insisted that both the employees and the investors have the same voting rights. We trusted him. Unfortunately, he began rallying the employees behind the scenes and also began bringing in his friends to replace the original Board members.

After the votes were counted, he and I were the only original Board members to be re-elected. The new Board members consisted of employees of the bank, a real estate agent (who was an agent for the bank), a non-investor and his friends. I soon learned that money and power could breed jealousy, greed and hatred.

H.A.P.P.Y.L.I.F.E.

It dawned on me that this person was playing a game of politics, not of fairness. I disagreed with his intentions and practices. He disrespected himself by being unfair to others.

I could see that the jealousy, greed and hatred of his actions were hurting the principle of our bank from within its own walls, and I did not want to be part of it. I resigned as Chairman of the Board.

When we are involved in any unfair practices, it will burden our shoulders, it will burden our heart and it will burden our soul. It may not be felt immediately, but eventually it will take its toll.

Jealousy, greed and hatred are a part of life, however, they do not have to be a part of our life. When we rid ourselves of these burdensome emotions, we can move on in our lives and continue to pursue happiness.

H.A.P.P.Y.L.I.F.E.

The Uncle Who Hit The Jackpot

A few years ago, I employed an assistant manager whose uncle had just won the lottery. She was extremely excited at first and we were all happy for her and her uncle. Soon, she started complaining to everyone that her uncle was not sharing his fortune with her family. She resented this and felt unhappy every day.

Finally, I asked her to think about the situation differently. What if she had won instead of her uncle? Would she have shared her winnings with him? After some thought, she told me that she probably would not because her uncle is well off.

I said to her, "Your husband has a great job, you have a steady income and you have beautiful children. You own a nice home. Your uncle probably thinks that you are well off too." I asked her not to feel bad that her uncle had not shared his good fortune with her. I encouraged her to take her uncle out and celebrate his good fortune.

I gave her a small bonus so that she could treat her uncle and celebrate his good luck. As it turned out, her uncle did end up sharing some of his winnings with her. He also bought her family a new entertainment center as a Christmas gift.

Ancient Wisdom taught us "we should treat others the way we would like to be treated." Allowing ourselves to succumb to the poison of greed and jealousy only breeds resentment and anger towards those we love. By sharing our thoughtfulness and gracefulness, we will turn our negative feelings toward others into a happy ending.

H.A.P.P.Y.L.I.F.E.

Listen to Our Stomach

If you've ever been to a buffet restaurant you can understand the saying "our eyes are always bigger than our stomachs." The endless rows of appetizers, salads, meats, and desserts are tempting. We continue to fill our plates with all of the food we want to sample. We always leave the table feeling overweight and uncomfortable.

There is a Chinese proverb that says, "Your stomach is the most fair judge." If we are full, we cannot eat any more. Our stomach knows our limitations and when we should be satisfied, but sometimes we desire more than we can handle.

Saying "no" to our fourth or fifth helping (and the temptation to get more) means we have finally learned how to be satisfied. Being satisfied means we have resisted greed and we are happy.

Having more does not always make us content. Out of luck, a poor man went to see a fortune-teller in hopes of hearing some good news. The fortune-teller looked at her smoky crystal ball and smiled. She told him, years from now, he would be much happier. Excited, the man asked, "So, you mean I'm going to be rich?" "No", she said, "you will just grow accustomed to being poor."

There is a Chinese proverb that tells us, "Regardless of who you are or how much you have, if you are satisfied, you are happy." More is not always better. We must be fair to our stomachs and to ourselves. When we work with our heart and soul, and are content with what we have, we can live a healthy and happy life.

H.A.P.P.Y.L.I.F.E.

The Real Estate Sand Trap

I have dealt with many tragedies and losses in my lifetime. I have experienced unfairness just like many others, particularly in some of my commercial real estate ventures. In my early thirties, I refinanced a piece of property that I owned, and used the proceeds to acquire an additional property for investment purposes.

I made a request to the county government and asked them to consider one of my investment properties as a commercial node in the County's Comprehensive Development Plan. In other words, I asked the county to consider my property for potential business development sites.

The county government asked me if they could use portions of my land to serve a nearby subdivision, free of charge, to solve their drainage problem. This is known as an easement. I complied with their request. I also allowed them to begin planning a water retention basin on my land, also free of charge. In total, I dedicated three to four acres of land to the county.

Because the land I purchased was in a relatively rural area, I understood that the county would not develop it for some time. I took matters into my own hands and turned the property into a sports facility. This complex offered a miniature golf course, batting cages, a banquet room, a driving range, a video game room, a large general game room, a pro shop, a playground and a snack bar.

During a meeting with the county government body, my attorney and I were told about the location of the proposed water retention basin on the land that

H.A.P.P.Y.L.I.F.E.

I had dedicated to the county. It was in an area that was inconvenient to my future development. I asked them if they could move it closer to the subdivision.

The county refused, saying it would cost the county more money. When I insisted, one member of the public works department told us that if I did not comply with the county's request, I would not be able to acquire my occupancy permit for my sport center. It meant I could not open for my business.

Young and inexperienced, I told them, "If I want to donate to a charity, I am happy to do so, but if someone puts a gun to my head and demands a donation, they will not get a dime!"

I regret what I said. I should have said, "I understand your point, Sir. I am sure we can work things out."

My unfriendly remark may have earned me severe headaches and setbacks. My business plan was to have the sports complex opened in the early spring to capture the business of the sports season. For whatever reasons, I did not receive my occupancy permit until late July, over halfway through the summer and sport season. The delayed opening caused the facility to open with incredible deficits that we were never able to overcome.

The county then approved a new subdivision even closer to my property. They asked me to dedicate more land and fund a two-lane public road connecting my property to the new neighborhood, which was extremely costly. I reluctantly agreed and complied with their request.

This came back to haunt me, as the driving range of my sports complex was facing the road. Even though I installed a large fence and netting, golfers would often hit the golf balls over the fence onto the road, sometimes hitting cars. I had to pay for the damages.

For the safety of the general public, I decided to close the sports complex, losing everything I had invested. I started to market my land to sell it for other usage.

Though I felt that the circumstances were unfavorable, I persisted and worked hard to improve my situation. Sometimes things happen to us that are unfair. We must accept these circumstances and continue to live our lives.

Through these hard times, I still had many loans to repay. When my land was up for sale, my first potential purchaser was a church. I was very excited about this sale, as it would eliminate my current debt.

Some county officials did not support this sale, since churches did not create tax revenues for the county. I continued to struggle financially.

Through the years, for different reasons and various circumstances, the county denied all of the other proposed developments of retirement homes, townhouses and a shopping center that included a movie theater.

I thought my struggles were finally over when I was approached by a new developer requesting to build a mixed-use project on my property, meaning there would be neighborhoods and commercial businesses. Before the deal was completed, the economy started to crumble. My purchaser could not get financing and dropped my project.

H.A.P.P.Y.L.I.F.E.

Currently, my property is under the rezoning process again. Some of the county officials wanted me to bring back the theater group and the commercial development project. In today's economic climate, it is difficult to put together a project of this magnitude in a way that will benefit all parties.

Needless to say, I am caught between politics and bureaucracy as I continue to face challenges and major financial losses. I feel like I am stuck in a sand trap and will never get out of this situation. Is what happened to me fair? Of course not! Should I stop trying? Of course not!

In contrast, I am motivated to try harder and maintain a positive attitude. Even though I may disagree with someone's opinions and practices, I continue to respect them and work with them out of fairness.

My mother once told me, "You may disagree or disapprove of what others believe and do, but you must respect them as human beings." That helped me to understand life better. While life may not always be fair to us, we must be fair in life.

I'm sure that some of you are experiencing your own hardships and unfair difficulties. Instead of writing off our situation as "unfair," we must recognize life's unfairness and move on. Keep working and never give up on getting out of your own "sand traps" in life. Better days are sure to come.

Regardless of what happens to myself, and my future, I want to thank everyone that has come across my path in life. Regardless of my wealth or state of my life, I will commit myself to serve the general public and our community with my best ability.

"It Is Fair, Dad"

I helped my oldest son start his own business when he was in his early twenties. I was at a point in life where I was able to support him as he started a computer business. He worked hard to overcome many obstacles and challenges, and is now very happy. I was also able to help my daughter go into business for herself. Despite the fact that her jewelry store did not last, I was able to provide her the opportunity.

I currently find myself in a different economic situation, in which I am not able to help my youngest son, Ken, establish himself in his chosen field, as I have done with my other children. I told him how sorry I was and how I felt it was unfair that I could not help him in the same way I helped his siblings.

"It is fair, Dad" was Ken's response. What he told me warmed my heart. He said to me. "Dad, you and Mom have given me everything that I would ever need to be successful in life. You raised me. You loved me. You gave me my education. You gave me my morals. You helped build my foundation to be a better person and a better man. For that, I love you and thank you."

My youngest son felt he had received as much as his siblings. He also said, "You and Mom gave me what is important. You gave me your love." He hugged me and tears were in our eyes.

Ken knows that I have tried my best to help him and others. I gave him the best education, caring and love. I have shared my life experiences with him. I will always be there to cheer for his successes and give him my love and support when he needs me.

H.A.P.P.Y.L.I.F.E.

I want to thank my son for allowing me to learn an important lesson. Life is not about how much money you can offer to others. It's about the value of the teaching, caring, and love you give them.

Whether life is fair or unfair is based on our perspective. Things happen for a reason and we must accept them as a fact of life.

By better understanding the principle of fairness, we are able to overcome adversity and appreciate our life experience. By searching further, we are able to view our life objectively from a new perspective to find the silver lining that is there waiting for us.

Why Me?

A good friend of mine named David once told me that the word "unfair" is not in his family's dictionary. His statement is so loud and clear that it allows me to view life in a new perspective.

A man is driving on the highway. He is speeding, but driving with the flow of traffic. Yet many cars continue to pass him. He is the only one who is pulled over and given a ticket by the police. Why him?

A widow, who lost her husband to cancer, has just received news that her daughter has also been diagnosed with the disease. Why her?

Events and tragedies happen to each one of us randomly. When things get tough, it is easy to think that your life is full of misfortune. You might even ask yourself, "why me?" and forget that unfortunate events happen to everyone. Some people get traffic tickets, while others speed but never get pulled over by the police. Some people are born into poverty while others know only wealth and luxury. Some people suffer from disease while others lose their homes, jobs or loved ones.

While tragedies may be unfair, they are a part of life. We must accept this as a fact of life and move on. To do so, we need to have a positive attitude, exercise patience, strive to improve and resist comparing ourselves to others. Life may be unfair, but we must be fair in life. It's not what life makes out of you, but what you make out of life.

H.A.P.P.Y.L.I.F.E.

When I was young, I believed I knew everything. That was so wrong. The fact is that the more I learn, the more I realize how little I really know.

When I was sick with cancer, I started to realize that some of the things I was pursuing (such as money) were things I might not ever be able to enjoy. There is always the unknown. It was at that time, I learned the true meaning of love when I needed it the most.

It is important to strike a balance between "seeking what you want" and "appreciating what you have". We must take steps to achieve our goals, but we cannot allow ourselves to be overtaken by jealousy or greed. We need to realize our limitations and appreciate what we already have (be it in our stomach or in our life!).

My life is full of obstacles, challenges, failures and business disasters. I had once said that I felt bulletproof not because I'm invincible, but because my body is full of holes. I could easily ask the same question, "Why me?" but my life experiences and common sense taught me that I needed to look at my life from various angles and appreciate it from different perspectives.

Had I never been diagnosed with cancer, I would never have taken off more time from work to spend with my family and been able to appreciate their love. If my commercial real estate business had succeeded, I may not have had the honor and the opportunity to write this book in which I have learned, and enjoyed, so much.

H.A.P.P.Y.L.I.F.E.

I am grateful for all my experiences and setbacks, even though some of those events could be viewed as unfair. I understand that for good, bad or worse, life is nothing but an experience.

I have made many mistakes throughout my lifetime, yet I harbor no regret. I understand that each experience has led me down the path to where I am today; which is "happy". I realize that having balance in life is as important as anything else.

Why me? We may never have a good answer for "why me?" but we certainly can improve our outlook with a positive attitude and a better understanding of life. Ancient Wisdom teaches us "living hard is much better than not living". That saying is very similar to our Modern Philosophy that says, "any day is better than no day at all."

We own and share the sky, the sun, the ocean, the forest, the mountains, the air we breathe and every raindrop that falls on earth. We all have experiences (both good and bad), feelings and love for everything we encounter, but we often don't realize how valuable they are until we have an open mind and see them for the treasures they are.

It is easy for us to ask ourselves, "Why me?" We often forget all of the wonderful things in life, and in nature, that we can enjoy and share with others.

I will never complain again. The question to myself is no longer "Why me?" nor "Why not me?" My new perspective is now "Please include me!"

H.A.P.P.Y.L.I.F.E.

Education

Education is the source of knowledge. Sharing knowledge creates a positive rippling effect that benefits mankind.

Ancient Wisdom
"Learning is infinite, knowledge is endless."

Modern Philosophy
"The children are our future."

H.A.P.P.Y.L.I.F.E.

Don't Live In A Home Without A Roof

I view education as two entities, learning and teaching. Life is sometimes hard. In order to get through it we must learn from our experiences. Then, we must share our wisdom with younger generations.

I once was talking to my friend who is also a banker. We were on the subject of investments when I asked him what he thought was the most valuable investment that anyone could make. He looked at me and said, "Well, that's simple, *education*." The cost of college is always increasing, but the value of a degree is always so much more. Learning is how we improve our place in life. I agree with my friend completely.

When I was asked to speak to the high school students, I wanted to encourage them to continue their education. I gave this analogy; college is usually only four years and based on a life expectancy of 80 years, the time it takes to earn a bachelor's degree is approximately five percent of your life. In turn, a degree will benefit your life for the next 60-plus years to come. Think of education as building a house. The twelve years you've already spent in the educational system is the foundation that supports everything that follows. The additional years spent in college or trade school is adding the roof, making the house functional and livable. When you are able to finish college, your "home" is completed.

Education is so important in our lives. It broadens our minds. It gives us a better understanding of the world around us and it makes our lives so much better. Please don't live in a home without a roof!

H.A.P.P.Y.L.I.F.E.

Elephants Teach

A few years ago, my wife and I went to Asia for a vacation. We took a tour through an elephant garden in Thailand. A gorgeous lake on one side and a tropical rolling hill on the other surrounded the resort. Large bright clouds were hanging high in the beautiful blue sky. The atmosphere was very peaceful and relaxing.

We were given the opportunity to ride on an elephant's back through a gorgeous meadow. Before we stepped on the platform to mount our elephant, we passed a fruit stand selling tropical bananas. The price was only fifty cents for an entire bundle, a huge bundle! We had to take advantage of such a bargain!

Happily eating our newly purchased bananas, we boarded the elephant and began our journey. An elephant jockey accompanied us and we offered some of our bananas to him. With a giggle and a shy smile, he shook his head.

As the elephant started walking, I asked the jockey if I could share a few of my bananas with the elephant. As soon as I handed some of the bananas to him, the elephant's trunk immediately shot back and snatched the bananas from our jockey's hand. The elephant's reaction was so robotic it shocked us.

To our surprise, the elephant suddenly stopped walking. I witnessed the jockey make several moves to encourage the elephant to start walking again, but to no avail. The jockey whipped the elephant once, twice and then three times but with no response from the elephant. We were stuck on a downhill slope looking for help.

H.A.P.P.Y.L.I.F.E.

I noticed that the train of elephants in front of us was getting further ahead, while the elephants behind us were encroaching upon us quickly. We began to worry.

Hoping to motivate the elephant to move forward, I gave our entire bundle of bananas to the jockey to feed the elephant. With the same reaction time, the elephant's trunk reached behind and snatched the bananas from the jockey's hand. To our relief, the elephant started walking again.

As we continued traveling, I noticed that there were hundreds of banana trees bordering the path. Tons and tons of bananas were all over the grounds nearby. I suddenly realized why the jockey had giggled when I offered him some of my bargain bananas. The bundle we bought was sold with the intent of feeding the elephants, not us humans.

Beyond college and other educational channels, we can learn valuable lessons through living. We can benefit from the lessons that we observe in our surroundings and through our circumstances.

Life truly is a learning experience. Regardless of what we do and how much we know, there is always something more for us to learn, even from an elephant. We learn as we go.

H.A.P.P.Y.L.I.F.E.

Turtles Fly

I have fallen many times in my life. Each time, I was able to get back up. The more I fell, the stronger I became. Life is not about winning or losing, it is about learning and experiencing. Whatever we choose to do in life, regardless of how it turns out, something positive can always be learned.

There once was a mother and father bird that hatched a family of baby birds. They also adopted a baby turtle and raised him like their own. One day they said to their children, "You must learn to fly and be independent. Life is only free and enjoyable if you know how to fly." Their children started practicing immediately.

They climbed to a tall branch, jumped off and flapped their arms. The young birds caught on very quickly; they were flying by the end of the week. The turtle, however, always fell to the ground.

Each morning the turtle awoke before his brothers and sisters to practice. He climbed the tree, edged to the end of the branch and flapped his arms. Each time he landed on the ground with a loud thud. After several weeks, he overheard his parents talking while he was resting behind a tree nearby.

"We should tell our little turtle that he has no wings and will never learn to fly." At that, the turtle walked out from behind the tree.

"Mom," he exclaimed, "don't say I will never learn! Do you know how much faster I can climb trees now? And when I fall I don't feel pain anymore! I haven't learned to fly yet, but I have learned many other valuable skills!"

H.A.P.P.Y.L.I.F.E.

We should look for opportunities to learn in every situation. Even when we fail, we can learn from our attempts. Each time that we make an attempt and learn from the experience, (no matter if it's good or bad) we will continue to improve our abilities, and ourselves, in the process.

We need to take our failures as shortcuts to success. We should enjoy our journey wherever it might take us. As the young turtle shows us, whether you are flying or falling, as long as you are trying, your life experience has been enriched.

H.A.P.P.Y.L.I.F.E.

Chopsticks

One of the most important lessons we can learn is to use what we have and what we know, in inventive ways. When we find ourselves with few possessions or skills, we should look for different opportunities to use what we already have. In doing so, we will be able to use the right tools that we already have and exercise our options to conquer our obstacles and challenges. This is especially important if we experience economic hardships.

Years ago, my father and I hosted a Chinese New Year party at one of our restaurants. Several notable dignitaries were invited to join our friends in the party; including Virginia Governor, Mills Godwin.

One of the main courses we served was Lobster Szechwan. I noticed that Governor Godwin was struggling to eat the lobster with his fork and knife, so I suggested he try his chopsticks. He seemed baffled by this suggestion. "How could I eat my meal easier with chopsticks than I can with my fork and knife?" he asked.

"Not your utensil chopsticks," I said. "Your natural chopsticks - your fingers!"

Governor Godwin listened and smiled. He started taking charge of the food with his own hands. As he put the juicy lobster meat into his mouth, he said, " Wow, that's delicious!"

We don't always need new possessions to enrich our lives or the exact skills to solve our problems. Instead, we can use what we already have, and use it in creative ways, to solve problems. It is this type of innovation that unlocks new dimensions of knowledge and education.

A revered Chinese poet and artist named Leum Man Choy proved this to the world when he integrated art, poetry and math together for the first time.

Leum was invited by a group of high government officials to join a party. He had been asked to create a poem that described a celebrated piece of artwork, titled *The Hundred Birds*. The painting depicted a pair of Phoenix birds and 98 other birds flying above a field.

(A typical poem in China includes four lines and each line contains seven words)

A bird born one after the other.

Three, four, five, six, seven, eight birds.

The world is full of different birds.

They eat all of our rice crops.

After the nobles and guests read the poem, they were very confused. This was not Leum Man Choy's best work, they thought, because it did not make sense. Seeing their confusion, Leum Man Choy explained his poem.

The first line, "One bird after another equals two" describes the two Phoenix birds.

H.A.P.P.Y.L.I.F.E.

The second line, " Three, four, five, six, seven, eight birds" describes the calculation of (3 times 4) plus (5 times 6) plus (7 times 8.). When you add 12 plus 30 plus 56 it equals 98. That describes the other ninety-eight birds in the painting.

The third line illustrates that there are many different kinds of birds in the world, just as there are many different kinds of people.

The fourth line describes the birds' eating habits as they fly over our rice fields.

The people began to understand. The poem matched the painting perfectly and they praised him for his work.

One of the guests said to Leum, "You are such a great poet. Your beautiful poem will further your reputation and be admired by many."

Leum replied humbly, " It is my honor to be part of this fantastic event and be able to serve its purpose."

The governor smiled and stated, "Your honor is our honor. The painting's value has just improved dramatically because of your beautiful poem."

The guest said, "Leum pierced two birds with one arrow."

Everyone in the party laughed and cheered with admiration.

Leum was not only a great poet, but also an intelligent mathematician. He combined his skills and knowledge to establish new forms of understanding. We should strive to do the same.

When we incorporate our knowledge and skills in different ways, we create new ideas to share with our peers and educate future generations.

H.A.P.P.Y.L.I.F.E.

Running Out Of Yardsticks

When I was a teenager, my mother always taught me to respect and embrace teachers as important stewards for our children. We must gain knowledge and learn life lessons from them. We need to have a better understanding of right and wrong and pass along this knowledge to the next generation.

I have learned a lot from the teachers in my life, and now I truly understand my mother's wisdom. I have kept in touch with many of my teachers throughout the years because I greatly appreciate their dedication, hard work, and love for their students.

One day, one of my best friends, Joe, a high school English teacher, came to visit me. He asked if I would consider talking to his students about the value of education.

He said, "Chin, some of my students are considering calling it quits after high school. I have tried to explain to them about the value of continuing their education, without success. I feel like I could talk to them all day long until I'm blue in the face, and they still would not be listening to my advice. The fact is I think the students would benefit by hearing from an outside expert."

I said, " You have a good point!"

Joe said, "I came here today to ask you to be that expert and see if you would be willing to come to the school and motivate my students. I said, "I would be delighted. It would be my honor to serve your students."

H.A.P.P.Y.L.I.F.E.

I was joyful to accept this challenge and greatly appreciated this opportunity to serve the students and my community. I knew that I had an important task ahead of me and I promised myself that I would not disappoint the students, their teacher or their school.

We talked about the value of education and I asked Joe why he became a teacher. He said, "Chin, I love my students and I love my job. I have never felt more fulfilled by a career in my entire life. Thankfully, I feel I am finally doing exactly what I am supposed to be doing with my life. In fact, if someone offered me a million dollars to change careers, I would graciously decline."

I said, "Joe, I don't know how much a million one-dollar bills means to you. If we could put them together end to end, they may stretch from Richmond, Virginia to Washington, D.C., which is a whole lot!"

He said, "Even if I won the lottery, Chin, I would not trade places with anyone." I said to myself, "How could you measure the love and dedication of this teacher with a yardstick?"

I am sure many teachers share the same sentiments as my friend Joe. My prior teachers, such as Betty, Leung, Fleming, Mangum, and many others, have demonstrated to me that most teachers are caring, dedicated, and committed to their students and their education. The teachers' contribution to our education, our society and to the history of mankind are so great that I am running out of words for praise and yardsticks for measurement.

H.A.P.P.Y.L.I.F.E.

A Fable I Once Read

Once we have learned our lessons, it is important to share them with others. I am sharing my experiences with you so you can learn from my mistakes.

As a young father, I made sure to teach my children lessons at every opportunity. When one of my children made a mistake, I made sure I explained both the mistake and the lesson to all three of my children.

I told them because I was their father, I should be responsible for their mistakes as well. My children knew that when they made a mistake I would feel pain in my heart. We need to support and learn from each other's mistakes.

The quintessential importance of teaching is best illustrated by a fable I once read. Although I do not know the source or the exact details, I will do my best to paraphrase it.

There was once a little traveler who set out on a journey through a village. His mission on this voyage was to help people. Upon entering the village, a small girl approached him and said, "Mr. Traveler, I have no clothes for the winter. May I have yours?"

"Of course," the traveler replied happily. He took off his shirt and gave it to the girl. Smiling, the girl skipped away with the traveler's shirt. Little did he know that her family owned a clothing factory.

Soon thereafter, an old lady approached him. "Mister, I'm a very poor lady. I cannot work. Will you please give me some money?" she said. Without hesitating, the traveler gave her all of his money. As it turned out, she was the richest lady in the village.

H.A.P.P.Y.L.I.F.E.

As he continued on his journey, he passed by a tree and saw a shoeless carpenter working very hard. The traveler took off his own shoes and gave them to the carpenter. Finally, he came to an old man in front of a crowded market. The old man was not wearing any pants. The traveler quickly took off his own pants and gave them to the old man.

Now the traveler had no money and no clothes. He ran off into the depths of the forest where a goblin was waiting for him. "Young man," he said eerily, "you are poor and naked. I will give you clothes and money, but only if you allow me to eat you first!"

The traveler thought about this proposition. Finally, he said, "You've got a deal."

As the goblin started eating the traveler he said, "Ahahaha! You are a fool! I'm not giving you anything after I eat you!"

Tears streamed down the traveler's eyes as he said, "Well, thank you for your honesty. You are one of the few individuals who has spoken to me truthfully on my journey."

This is the end of the fable, but I like to add my own interpretations. Just like a fortune cookie with no fortune, I enjoy making my own endings.

As the traveler's body disappeared, his spirit rose to Heaven, where an angel greeted him. "Look at you," said the angel, "I'm sorry to see you like this - naked, poor and without a body." As they were speaking, the people in the village and the goblin were listening and laughing.

The traveler replied, "I gave to those in need. I gave my shirt to the girl not because she needed the clothing to keep her warm, but because she lacked confidence about her beauty. I gave my money to the old lady because even though she was rich, her heart was poor. The carpenter needed my shoes to continue his hard work, so I gave my shoes to him. The pants were given unconditionally to the old man because he needed to cover his own sins. I allowed the goblin to eat me because I wanted to trust him. I enjoyed my journey all the way to Heaven and I harbor no regrets."

Hearing this, the villagers became silent and some had tears in their eyes. They walked away with their heads bowed in honor of the wise traveler.

That next winter, long after the traveler went to Heaven, the little girl donated enough clothes to the needy so they would be able to survive the cold season. The rich old lady gave all of her wealth to build homes for the homeless. Her donation provided all the work that the shoe-clad carpenter could handle. The old man became a preacher and taught the children of the village how to be better people. And the goblin never told another lie. The traveler knew that with his sacrifices, he was teaching future generations.

There are events in our own lives that we may not understand at first, but with time, they evolve into understanding. The good that we are providing to others right now may never show us a positive result in our lifetime, but the impact will undoubtedly benefit generations to come.

If we are able to educate one person, we are tossing a stone into a lake. As the water ripples, our teachings are spreading to many.

H.A.P.P.Y.L.I.F.E.

Two Heads Are Better Than One

I consider myself a positive and hard working person. I am able to extrapolate the positive in any situation and I never give up on a task. My friends regard me as a problem solver and visionary, as they often come to me for advice. Regardless of these strengths, I have found that I need help more often than not.

In the midst of writing this book, I knew that I needed help. As I was unskillful with computers, I placed an ad for a typist. I interviewed a college student named Megan. I was impressed with her nice personality and intellectual ability and I decided to hire her.

She was only able to work on my book for just a few short weeks because of college. But I got a lot more than I expected. Instead of being just my typist, she gave me a lot of good advice and became my friend. We bounced ideas off each other and she offered me numerous suggestions to better organize my stories. We made an incredible team.

If you enjoy reading this book, please help me thank Megan for her contribution. She added a lot of color to my stories.

I was open to Megan's ideas and was rewarded with an abundance of new knowledge. I also improved my writing skills. I think Megan learned a bit from my experience and perspectives as well. It is important for us to know our strengths and weaknesses. As long as we are willing to learn, there is always room for improvement.

Knowledge can be measured as if it were in a glass. If we feel like we know everything, then the glass is filled to the brim. There is no room for improvement.

In reality, knowledge is endless. We can learn from everything. When our glass gets full, we must continue to improve and "enlarge our glass" in order to retain additional knowledge. If not, the education that we receive will overflow and spill over our glass onto the table, never to be contained. We will be unable to make the best use of our knowledge.

We must learn from each other and benefit from the lessons we are taught. As Ancient Wisdom teaches us, "Learning is infinite, knowledge is endless." We should never be satisfied with how much we have learned. We must strive to share our knowledge with others in order to fully benefit mankind.

H.A.P.P.Y.L.I.F.E.

Write Your Own Fortune

I once hosted a dinner for a group of friends and dignitaries. As we were enjoying the dessert, Governor Godwin of Virginia opened his fortune cookie and exclaimed, "Where is my fortune?"

I turned to my lawyer friend sitting next to me and said jokingly, "Defend me on this one!" Smiling, he replied, "I didn't make the cookies, you did." The guests laughed at my situation.

Running out of options, I stood up and said, "Ladies and Gentlemen, Governor Godwin had the best fortune cookie." I paused and said, "His fortune cookie has no fortune in it, but now he can write his own fortune."

Everyone in the room laughed and cheered, knowing that we did not need a good fortune to have fun and to enjoy ourselves.

I am very thankful, and it is my great honor, to be able to share my thoughts, stories, perspectives and life experiences with you. I hope that you enjoyed reading this book and found it cheerful and useful. Now you can go out and create your own fortune and find your happiness.

In reference to the Emperor's choice in the beginning of the book, you may already have your own answer. Forgive me though; I often have my own perspective and interpretations.

The Emperor knew the flawless jade was perfect in shape and color and was of the highest quality. He would choose this precious jade for his wife.

However, the worn jade caught his eyes. As he looked closer, the Emperor discovered the inner beauty of this jade. He appreciated its strength and sacrifice. He also valued its experience and longevity. His country needed this jade as its symbol because the worn jade represented power, success, tradition and the history of his country.

A wise man once told us, "We need to search for the hidden meaning to discover the true lesson." When you look closer and think deeper, you will find the answer is that a **H.A.P.P.Y.L.I.F.E.** is within your reach.

Life is imperfect. But that does not prevent us from being chosen by a higher being. Everyone is created equal in life and every person has value and purpose. Regardless of who we are, or how imperfect we seem, we are not prevented from living a happy life.

Explore, dream, discover, learn, and share your experience by *H*elping others, having a positive *A*ttitude, exercising *P*atience, fostering *P*assion, saying *Y*es we can, learning to *L*ove, aiming for *I*mprovement, understanding *F*airness and valuing *E*ducation.

Now go out and live a **H.A.P.P.Y.L.I.F.E.**

Special Acknowledgement

To my family and friends;

I want to thank my parents, my wife, my family and friends for their love, teachings, and support. Everyone who has come across my path in life has shaped my wonderful experience and has allowed me to enjoy a happy life that I greatly appreciate.

I want to thank Dewayne, Megan, Eric, Mike, Ken, Justin at JCL Design, Steele Insurance Agency, Robert and Brandylane Publishers, and others who helped me bring this book to fruition.

To the students of the local high school;

Your approval of my speech and your valuable comments on my message about enjoying a happy life moved me to write this book. Your appreciation has inspired me to devote myself to helping others to live their own happy life. You have offered me a new mission and higher purpose. Thank you for renewing my passion.

To honor your encouragement that motivated me to write this book, I plan to donate copies of this book to libraries and charities. A portion of the income from the sale of this book will be used to benefit students through scholarships and other means.

I will continue to promote the concept of H.A.P.P.Y.L.I.F.E. and emphasize the importance of education for the benefit of today's society and for future generations.

H.A.P.P.Y.L.I.F.E.

Letters from the teacher and the students

"In the spring of 2009, my school and I invited Mr. Thick Chin to speak to five 12th grade English classes.

As their teacher, I was trying to impress upon my students the importance of continuing their education after high school. Unfortunately, my efforts were falling on deaf ears and I felt that the message to the students could be better delivered by an outside source.

I knew exactly who would be my motivational expert, my "ace-in-the-hole", who could effectively reach my students.

Mr. Chin has always been an inspiration to me and I was certain he could inspire my students, as well. We were not disappointed. Mr. Chin was up to the task and performed spectacularly.

After Mr. Chin spoke, I asked my students to evaluate his lecture as a homework assignment. Frankly, I was stunned by many of their responses, even humbled. My students soaked up Mr. Chin's wisdom like sponges.

I was so touched by their responses that I copied their evaluations and gave them to Mr. Chin. I told him, "Mr. Chin, your impact on my students was tremendous…take a look at these letters"

Joseph B. Allred, Teacher
Henrico High School

H.A.P.P.Y.L.I.F.E.

"I really enjoyed the lecture that Mr. Chin gave us the other day. It was really inspirational and had a lot of truth. I liked his example that we must always improve. I believe in education as well.

One thing I noticed is that all of Mr. Chin's principles interconnect with each other and are related. I think that this was a clever acronym and I applaud Mr. Chin for his efforts." -D.J.

"I really enjoyed Mr. Chin's visit and would love to have him back. He came off really nice, very respectful. He had a lot to share, especially his life.
He said a lot about education and realizing what it is and how important it is in life. It stood out to me when he talked about the 12-year foundation we have already built in school. I never looked at it like that before.

He is a spiritual man and his testimony made me feel like life isn't as hard as I think or make it out to be. He also made me feel like I could conquer just about anything after all he went through.

Mr. Chin is a wonderful man and speaker. I would love to have him back again. He is very inspirational and I liked to listen to him talk through his 'THICK CHIN'" -M.E.

"The way Mr. Chin came into the classroom and started the conversation was quite interesting, and is what made it awesome. I was quite shocked about how comfortable he seemed...the way he explained everything was excellent.

Overall he is one of those speakers who seemed to do that as a full-fledged job." -C.K.

"Mr. Chin was inspirational, a natural motivational speaker. The entire presentation really moved me. Every factor of his 'mission statement' was something of an eye-opener...It made me want to rethink my life...Anyone can gain perspective if they take time to listen." -E.M.

"Mr. Chin really made me think about my attitude and how I need to have better patience. I really did learn that I needed to be just a little more patient because you never know what kind of day someone else is having." -C.R.

"I believe that Mr. Chin's presentation was very constructive, and it gave me a better outlook on life." -T.C.

"I felt like Mr. Chin and I had a lot in common based on our background. We both came from third world places where living is hard. We didn't have real opportunities as we do here in the US. We both came here not speaking English, and we learned it.

Mr. Chin has been through a lot. He has made mistakes and has learned from them. That is what made him who he is. It's hard to really understand the life of somebody like him unless you have lived in the same position or have known him for a long time. You just can't live without experiences. You can't get better without practicing.

His story inspired me to keep working hard until I can't any more. Thank Mr. Allred for inviting Mr. Chin to come speak to our class." -C.R.

H.A.P.P.Y.L.I.F.E.

"Mr. Chin's visit was very touching. His HAPPYLIFE method is very true in becoming successful in life. I believe if someone were to follow it, they would live a happy life and never work a day in their life.

I think Mr. Chin should continue speaking to young students and inspiring them not to give up and 'Yes, we can.' "   -D.S.

"When Mr. Chin came to talk to us on Friday, I did not expect it to be as wonderful as it was. He really made me think about my attitude and how I need to have better patience.

I also thought it was really sweet that he felt like it was an honor to meet us…I really did learn a lot of knowledge and understanding from his speech. I would love, and be honored, if he came back another day and taught more about his country and his language."   -C.R.

"Last Friday, a speaker came to our English class to speak to us. His name was Mr. Chin. He was very polite and nice. He spoke to us about his culture, heritage and where he grew up. He was so happy, full of joy and proud of where he came from and what he's doing with his life.

I cried after I heard his stories. Mr. Chin inspired me to never give up on achieving my goals. We must always think positive with a positive attitude. Mr. Chin made a very good point about love. Without love, there will be no happiness in life."   -V.R.

To my readers;

      Thank you for allowing me to share my life experiences with you. I hope that this book enriched your life and helped you to find a new perspective about happiness.

      Please share your comments and suggestions to improve this book. If you enjoyed reading it and think that my book would be helpful to others, please kindly refer this book to your family and friends.

      I would be proud to have you think of me as a friend. I hope I will have the honor of shaking your hand and thank you in person one day.

Best Wishes,

T.S. Chin

The author is available to speak at schools, charity groups, civic organizations, businesses, churches and fundraising events about the importance of education and how to live a Happy Life.

    Visit us at: **www.HappyLifeBook.com**

    Email us at: **HappyLifeBook@yahoo.com**